ISBN 978-0-364-67576-2
PIBN 11273452

For support please visit www.forgottenbooks.com

1 MONTH OF
FREE
READING

at

www.ForgottenBooks.com

By purchasing this book you are eligible for one month membership to ForgottenBooks.com, giving you unlimited access to our entire collection of over 1,000,000 titles via our web site and mobile apps.

To claim your free month visit:

www.forgottenbooks.com/free1273452

Historic, archived document

Do not assume content reflects current
scientific knowledge, policies, or practices.

FORESTS AND
NATIONAL PROSPERITY

A REAPPRAISAL OF THE FOREST SITUATION
IN THE UNITED STATES

Forest Service

U. S. DEPARTMENT OF AGRICULTURE

Miscellaneous Publication No. 668

FORESTS AND NATIONAL PROSPERITY

A Reappraisal of the Forest Situation

in the United States

Foreword

TODAY, THE NEED for productive forests transcends that of any earlier period. The Nation faces the double task of creating a lasting prosperity at home, and of working to improve economic conditions for people all over the world. Clearly, we shall need abundant resources for this task. The war pointed toward the heights of national productivity of which we are capable. It also cut deeply into our natural resources. We know now that the Nation can no longer be satisfied with the best achieved in the past. And it is equally clear that wise use of all our resources is vital if we are to reach the new, high goals ahead.

During 1945 and 1946 the Forest Service made a reappraisal of the forest situation in the United States. Its purpose was to bring up to date and amplify basic information on our timber resources, to interpret this information in relation to the national economy, and to reexamine national policies and needs in forest conservation. Previous analyses of a similar nature were made in 1938 and 1932.

Forests contribute to the welfare of the Nation in many ways. They are invaluable in the protection of watersheds; they afford recreation and sport for people in all walks of life; they are the habitat of many forms of wildlife; they provide range forage for millions of livestock. But this appraisal dealt mainly with the timber resource. Other aspects of the situation were considered primarily in relation to timber use.

The reappraisal has made use of the large amount of information available from the Forest Survey and other activities of the Forest Service, and from other agencies. Such information has been brought up to date, checked, and supplemented. Much new resource information also was obtained to assure an authoritative summary of the quantity, quality, distribution, growth, and drain of the timber resources in the United States proper. Only incidental attention was given to the forests of Alaska and to the world timber situation. Estimates of potential requirements for forest products and of unavoidable losses through natural causes were supplemented by consideration of margins for new uses, export, and national security.

Especially important new information on the character of forest practices and the degree of forest management by ownership classes was obtained by a field survey. The volume and character of wood waste and the possibilities of using more of it were explored. Problems of the timber industries in relation to raw-material supply were reviewed. The status and needs of forest protection were reexamined. Special attention was given to problems of ownership, because ownership so fundamentally influences the kind of action needed.

This report brings together in concise form the over-all findings of the reappraisal and restates the principal Federal measures which I believe are necessary to assure ample timber supplies for the future. Various aspects of the reappraisal are covered more fully in a series of separate reports, some of which have already been published.

The report shows that the Nation's saw-timber supply is declining and, of equal significance, its quality is deteriorating. Saw-timber cut plus losses from natural causes exceeds annual growth by 50 percent. Yet indications are that the intrinsic needs of the Nation for saw-timber products are considerably greater than present cut. Whether we are in for a permanent timber shortage or whether we shall have plenty of timber depends largely on what we do now. We have enough forest land. The challenge is to grow the timber.

A crop of wood cannot be grown in a single year like a crop of corn. Tomorrow's wood supply is in the trees growing in the forests today. Our forest growing stock, therefore, must be large enough so that as one year's crop is harvested, enough trees will be coming of age to provide the next year's crop. It is my hope that publication of this report will help spur the Nation to prompt, forceful, and comprehensive action to build up and maintain the forest resources so as to insure their maximum contribution to lasting prosperity for our country.

Lyle F. Watts

Chief, Forest Service.

Acknowledgments

THIS REAPPRAISAL was a Service-wide undertaking. A large group of the best-qualified administrative and research personnel in the several regions and in Washington participated. The project was conducted and the several reports prepared under the general direction of Assistant Chief R. E. Marsh, assisted by V. L. Harper. Much of the preliminary planning was done by Associate Chief E. H. Clapp, who retired before work got under way. The writing of this report was largely the work of R. E. Marsh, C. Edward Behre, and H. Glenn Meginnis. The list of those who took part in analyzing the Nation-wide data or in preparing reports also includes:

REED W. BAILEY	FRANK A. INESON
A. A. BROWN	LEONARD F. KELLOGG
W. R. CHAPLINE	L. F. KNEIPP
GARDNER H. CHIDESTER	PAUL E. MALONE
ALBERT C. CLINE	IRA J. MASON
LAKE F. COMPTON	E. T. MERRICK
ROBERT W. COWLIN	WARREN T. MURPHY
GEORGE W. CRADDOCK	LESLIE W. ORR [2]
RUSSELL N. CUNNINGHAM	KENNETH W. PARKER
WILLIAM A. DUERR	EARL S. PEIRCE
T. C. FEARNOW	JAY H. PRICE
R. D. GARVER	JAMES C. RETTIE
J. ALFRED HALL	JOHN H. SIEKER
ROBERT T. HALL	WILLIAM N. SPARHAWK
FRANK J. HALLAUER	LLOYD W. SWIFT
PERCY D. HANSON	CHARLES L. TEBBE
CARL HARTLEY [1]	H. BASIL WALES
W. R. HINE	ROBERT K. WINTERS
HOWARD HOPKINS	STEPHEN N. WYCOFF
S. BLAIR HUTCHISON	

In the compilation of basic statistics of land and timber stand, and in varying degree in other phases, the Forest Service had the cooperation of other Federal agencies, State foresters and other State officials, and the American Forestry Association, the latter having started an independent appraisal project in 1944. Many private organizations and individuals contributed in one way or another.

---

[1] Bureau of Plant Industry, Soils, and Agricultural Engineering.
[2] Bureau of Entomology and Plant Quarantine.

source of livelihood for millions of people. In 1946 it afforded work equivalent to 3.3 million full-time jobs and wages totaling 6.3 billion dollars.

Rural America has perhaps the most direct stake in productive forests. Countless small towns and communities are supported wholly or in large part by forest-based enterprises. Millions of rural people, including farmers, look to the forests for regular or part-time work and for simple products essential to their mode of living. To them, and to many people everywhere, well-managed forests mean steady jobs and permanent communities.

Productive forests are needed for much besides their timber. Today, more than ever, the Nation needs to protect its priceless soils and watersheds—to guard against floods, erosion, and damage to water supplies. It needs the livestock products from forest range, and it needs to utilize fully the great recreational and wildlife values of forest lands.

Yet our forests, for the most part, are not in good shape to meet these varied and compelling demands. Years of poor and destructive cutting, of fires, and lack of management have steadily reduced timber capital and impaired other products and services. Years of exploitation and a long concurrent history of rising prices to consumers spell timber scarcity, not abundance, today.

The need for better forestry is heightened by economic circumstances and new concepts growing out of the war and the reconversion. Wartime experience in production has given the Nation new and higher aims for peace. Foremost among these is the emphasis on achieving a stable, high-level economy and full employment as a matter of vital national policy. Maintenance of high national income, with jobs for all, is of the utmost importance if we are to avoid recurring cycles of "boom and bust."

A prosperous well-integrated economy implies, for one thing, productive forests capable of supplying a greater timber cut than heretofore visualized —and on a sustained basis. Indeed, it means full use of all basic resources, and concerted policies and action to conserve and keep them in good supply. America, in its bid for strength and prosperity, should face this issue squarely. Already we are a "have-not" nation with respect to certain minerals and are forced to compete increasingly for critical materials in the world market. We are using up our soils. We have made heavy inroads on the timber. Yet forests, which lie all around us and occupy one-third of our land area, are a renewable resource. Though depleted, they can be built up to supply fully the needs of a strong, growing nation.

Beyond the domestic situation, this country needs productive forests to meet new international obligations and to help establish the peace. A smaller world requires a closer harmonizing of world supplies and needs of basic materials. The world is short of softwood timber and the forests of North America are of key importance in world supply. It is in the national interest to build up America's forests so as to contribute in the long run to world timber trade just as it is to supply food and other necessities for rehabilitation now.

One fact stands out clearly: this country needs to produce and to use in full measure the products and services of its forests as a part of the larger obligation to gain a stable, prosperous economy and hence a better hope for world security. This, in brief, is the broad economic and social setting in which American forestry finds itself today.

Highlights of the Forest Situation

1. *The Nation has plenty of forest land.* Excluding Alaska, there is 624 million acres—one-third of the total land and about two-thirds of the original forest area. About 461 million acres is commercial, suitable and available for growing merchantable timber. The potential productivity of this vast domain is great—enough eventually to fill domestic needs generously, provide for national emergencies, and export to a world undersupplied with timber, as it is with food.

2. *The supply of all-important saw timber is steadily shrinking.* Originally there must have been 8,000 billion board feet or more. In 1945 there was about 1,601 billion. The difference plus what additional wood has grown in the meantime was used up or destroyed. The quantity of saw timber is still declining. In the 15 timber States for which

comparable Forest Survey data are available, containing 60 percent of the Nation's saw timber and accounting for almost three-fourths of the annual drain, the saw-timber stand declined 156 billion board feet (14 percent) in a period averaging 11 years prior to 1945.

3. *Our forests are operating in the red.* More timber is cut or destroyed each year than is replaced by growth. Saw timber is growing at an annual rate of about 35 billion board feet. But the 54-billion-board-foot annual drain by cutting and by natural losses in 1944—though well below the 60 billion board feet of the peak war years, 1941–43, and below that of 1946 and 1947—exceeded saw-timber growth by about 50 percent:

Section [1]	Growth (billion bd. ft.)	1944 drain (billion bd. ft.)	Drain ratio (percent)
North	8.4	9.0	108
South	19.9	24.9	125
West	7.0	20.0	285
United States	35.3	53.9	153

[1] For boundaries of sections referred to, see fig. 2, p. 14.

True, for all timber including that less than saw-timber size, there was a near balance between drain (13.7 billion cubic feet) and growth (13.4 billion). But there is little satisfaction in this because 80 percent of the drain is in saw timber, particularly the better softwoods, whereas much of the growth is in small low-grade trees and inferior hardwoods.

Because of the backlog of virgin timber, the overcut is not dangerous in the West, but continuation of the present rate and character of cutting in the East would sacrifice future productivity. Actually it is unlikely that the present drain in the East will continue, for obtaining suitable stumpage is increasingly difficult. But projecting 1944 drain 20 years ahead in all regions [1] (assuming no change in cutting practices) indicates a 27-percent reduction in our saw-timber stand by 1965. For the two leading timber-products regions—the Southeast and the Pacific Northwest—the decline would be 60 and 39 percent, respectively.

4. *Forest industries are feeling the pinch of timber shortages and declining quality.* Even in the West local timber shortages are already making themselves felt; in western Washington less than half the primary forest industries have enough private timber in sight to keep going more than a few years. In the South a horde of little sawmills are

[1] For boundaries of regions referred to, see fig. 2, p. 14.

logs for veneer and other specialty products. are especially hard hit. The expanding fir-plywood industry of the Northwest faces major readjustment before it has really hit its stride. Pulp and paper companies, though they can use small material, often meet stiff competition for softwood timber, particularly in the South, and in the North some face actual shortage.

Although much progress in achieving balance between plant and woods operations is being made, particularly by some pulp and lumber companies, the forest industries as a whole are not well geared to a sustained timber supply. They own little more than one-tenth of the commercial forest. Their operations generally are not adapted to complete, integrated use of the available timber. Plant capacity greater than tributary forests can sustain is still a threat to the growing stock in many localities.

5. *A flexible long-range goal for timber growth is proposed.* Careful study—looking beyond current limitations to long-range possibilities because forestry, like the Nation's growth, is a long-time affair—suggests a growth goal of 18 to 20 billion cubic feet annually, including 65 to 72 billion board feet of saw timber. This visualizes potential domestic requirements—the estimated quantity a fully employed, prosperous people might use if the timber were readily available at reasonable prices—of 61 billion board feet, which is more than the annual saw-timber cut of 55 billion in the prosperous years 1925–29, or that in the peak war years. The goal also includes a margin for irreducible losses, ineffective growth, new uses, and exports, and a backlog for national security. Setting the goal slightly higher or lower would make little difference in the program required to reach it. But to aim for much less than 72 billion board feet of saw timber annually would not be sound public policy or consistent with the responsibilities and needs of a large, growing nation.

6. *Attaining this goal means stepping up annual growth of all timber by one-half and doubling saw-timber growth.* This is a big order. For the Nation as a whole, forest growing stock is below par in quantity, quality, and distribution. About 35 percent (164 million acres) of the commercial forest area is deforested or has less than 40 percent of full stocking. Nearly half the commercial forest

of the growth goal.

Nationally, a 469-billion-board-foot deficit in the growing stock of the East is partially offset by the virgin timber of the West where two-fifths of the stands are as yet untouched. However, about one-fourth of the commercial forest area of the West has been reduced to seedling or sapling growth or is denuded, and the active growing stock of young timber is only about a third of that needed to reach the West's share of the goal.

7. *Clearly, the goals cannot be achieved for several decades.* It would be unrealistic to assume that good cutting practices will be generally applied within a few years, that adequate protection can be promptly achieved, that planting will be undertaken on a large enough scale to bring the bulk of the idle lands into production within a generation, that the construction of access roads into new areas will keep sufficiently ahead of the demand to relieve the pressure for overcutting elsewhere, or that cutting operations will be so located as to assure continuous high-level output locality by locality. But even if all these things could be accomplished, it is estimated that saw-timber growth would not reach 64 billion board feeet (the level of potential domestic requirements and losses) in less than 45 years. Moreover, if there were to be a good margin for national security, export, and the like, growing stock would have to be further built up for another 25 or 30 years. These calculations—in no sense forecasts—assume that for perhaps 30 years annual drain would be less than 50 billion board feet—some 4 billion below 1944, although output of major products since 1945 has actually been higher than in 1944.

8. *Meanwhile, the Nation cannot rely on increased imports.* There is a world shortage of timber, especially of softwoods for construction. Europe, largely self-sufficient in timber before the war, will need to import for years to come. The forests of Soviet Asia, the East Indies, and the Philippines are remote and mostly undeveloped; in the main they will go to supply the Orient. Central and South America and Africa can supply some hardwoods though little construction timber. Canada doubtless will continue to be our chief source of imports and possibly can furnish somewhat more pulp and paper, especially newsprint,

although her own supply of operable timber is diminishing. For 30 years or more the United States has imported more wood and wood products than it has exported. It can no longer rely as much on imports as in the past. The Nation must look mainly to its own forests.

9. *The forest situation, therefore, poses a dilemma.* The intrinsic needs of this country for saw-timber products are considerably greater than the present cut. Yet saw-timber drain already exceeds annual growth. To increase current output implies accelerating timber depletion and so hastening the day when drastic reduction in the use of timber products would be inescapable. To curtail output now so as to facilitate building up growing stock and annual growth would leave urgent needs (such as that for more housing) unfilled and might weaken the foundation for a high-level national economy. There is no wholly satisfactory way out.

The Nation should adopt a broader and more positive forest conservation program than has existed in the past. We need to stop forest destruction and deterioration, to put idle forest land to work, and to obtain widespread adoption of sustained-yield forest management in order to assure ample supplies of timber products for future generations. But to meet the pressing demands of the years just ahead, we should strive to keep national output of timber products from falling much below present levels, if possible.

10. *More efficient use of wood can help bridge the gap though it cannot decisively relieve the pressure on growing stock.* Wood waste—material from the forest which is not used for marketable products other than fuel—was estimated at 109 million tons for 1944, or over half of all timber cut. This waste can be reduced through more efficient logging and manufacturing; and by improved chemical recovery such as the processes for making alcohol from sawmill and pulping wastes. However, economic use cannot be made of all or even most of the wood now wasted. Opportunities are principally in the South and Pacific Northwest, where there are large primary plants and large usable concentrations of wood waste. Even though the use of wood waste will not greatly affect forest drain or alter requirements as visualized in the long-range growth goal, it can help meet current needs for wood and is important for other reasons. It strengthens the incentive for better and more diversified forestry. New uses for wood waste

also serve to expand employment and industrialization, and hence should help cushion the effects of forest depletion on dependent communities.

11. *Increasing the cut of virgin timber in the West would relieve the pressure on the growing stocks of the East.* Clearly, eastern forests are not in condition to go on bearing over 60 percent of the country's saw-timber drain. Some reduction of output appears inevitable. Good forest practices can hold this reduction to perhaps 15 or 20 percent, but even so, the growing stock would need to be built up for 20 or 30 years before output could be safely restored.

To help maintain national output, the cut of virgin timber in the West could be increased for a number of years. But this should not be at the expense of good forest practice. Operations should be properly located and cutting practices adapted to maintain forest productivity in each locality. Because of such considerations an increase of western output hinges largely on rapid construction of access roads into undeveloped country, particularly in the national forests.

12. *More than 30 percent of the Nation's saw timber is in the national forests.* Because private lands have been generally more accessible, a large part of the virgin timber still awaiting development is in the western national forests. It is largely to these forests that the Nation must look to minimize a prospective decline elsewhere in the output of timber products. To bring the output of all the national forests up to their sustained-yield capacity calls for more intensive management as well as a large road-building program. Timber sales need to be speeded up; more of the output should be from thinnings and other improvement measures in growing forests. Denuded areas should be planted. Better protection and more adequate administrative facilities should be provided. But output, working circle by working circle, should not be allowed to exceed sustained-yield capacity.

We can also turn to the national forests of Alaska, whose resources are as yet untapped on a large scale. Alaska's timber will be chiefly valuable to supplement our pulpwood supply. When the pulp and paper industry becomes established in Alaska it should be able to supply about 7 percent of the Nation's potential pulp and paper requirements— representing a cut of about 1½ million cords of pulpwood annually. We should make the most of this opportunity.

13. *But this country's forest problem centers*

public forests should increase.

14. *Private forests need much better protection.*
Fire continues to take a heavy toll despite the great progress in cooperative fire control begun in 1911. Organized protection was provided for 319 million acres in 1946, but much of this did not meet desirable standards. About one-fourth of the private land in need of organized protection, chiefly in the South and the Central region, is still without it.

Moreover, comparatively little has been done to curb insect pests and diseases, which take an even heavier toll of timber. As in fire control, it will take organized, collective action on a much more ample scale as contemplated in the Forest Pest Control Act of June 25, 1947, to cope adequately with these hazards.

15. *Timber-cutting practices on private lands, with some notable exceptions, are far from satisfactory.* Encouraging progress has been made in recent years, especially in the South, but about two-thirds of the cutting on private lands is still poor or destructive, and only 8 percent is up to really good forestry standards. The 51 million acres in some 400 properties of more than 50,000 acres each, chiefly lumber- and pulp-company holdings, receives the best treatment. About 39 percent of the cutting on these lands is on a sustained yield basis, and 29 percent is good or high order. But these large holdings comprise only 15 percent of the commercial forest land in private ownership. Three-fourths of it, about 261 million acres, is held by more than 4 million small owners in properties averaging only 62 acres each. About 71 percent of the cutting on this land, more than half of which is farm woodland, is poor or destructive.

16. *The small private holding is the toughest problem.* Many of the obstacles to better forestry stem from the huge number of these small properties; their small, often uneconomic, size; the diversity of aims and lack of skill with which they are handled; the instability of their ownership and management; the lack of capital and the pressure for current income. Yet the small holdings include much of the most accessible and potentially the most productive forest land. Practical means

under good management, the public, too, has a big stake in this. The public role should be to help minimize the handicaps, to encourage and assist, and to apply appropriate restraints to stop unnecessary forest destruction. Where handicaps are too great—particularly where forests are run-down and returns are small or long-deferred—or where benefits and services accrue mainly to the public at large, permanent public ownership and management is generally the answer. A large acreage now privately owned is in this category. But private forestry can succeed on the greater part of the land; there are examples now, in every region and among many classes of owners.

18. *American forestry has made great strides but there is still a big job to do.* We have the world's greatest public forest system—the national forests—with a large backlog of timber and other important values under stable and sound management. Other Federal forest lands have also been placed under management. State forestry activities have been steadily expanded and strengthened. Much progress has been made in protecting forests from fire. Research, on which the techniques and "know-how" of forestry depend, has made great headway, especially in recent years. We have the beginnings of an effective program of aids to small owners. A substantial acreage of private forests—mostly in the larger holdings—is under management and a growing number of owners are practicing good forestry. Many are buying more land for timber growing. And, among the hopeful factors, there are today's good markets and favorable economic climate which, if maintained and taken advantage of, can do much to advance the forestry movement. All these things augur well for the future.

Nevertheless, little more than a beginning has been made toward achieving a sound, permanent forest economy in this country. Clearly much remains to be done to strengthen and equip public forests for a greater output and to get good forestry on the great bulk of the private lands. A piecemeal attack, as at present, will not suffice. The Nation needs a comprehensive, unified forest policy and concerted action going far beyond anything accomplished in the past.

Action Needed

A reappraisal of this kind logically includes consideration of what action is needed. As the preceding pages have made apparent, the forest situation is extremely complex. It involves a great variety of physical and economic considerations. There is no panacea by which satisfactory forest conservation can be attained in this country.

For considering what is needed, a point of departure is afforded by the comprehensive program recommended by the Department of Agriculture in 1940 to the Joint Congressional Committee on Forestry, which had been commissioned by the President to investigate and report on the Nation's forest situation. Those recommendations and other proposals have been carefully reexamined in the light of the reappraisal findings, progress in the intervening years, and the current economic outlook. For example, after careful study it was concluded that incentive payments for good forestry practices do not form a sound major approach to forest conservation. As another example, the status of State forest-regulatory measures and other relevant circumstances were carefully reconsidered, and as a result the Forest Service continues its recommendation of a Federal-State plan of regulating cutting and other forest practices on forest land.

In presenting its program of action now, the Forest Service reaffirms the philosophy that forest conservation requires Federal, State, and local governments and private owners and agencies to act in effective cooperation. It takes into account the need for Federal leadership in many segments of the work. It further recognizes that although there is need for considerably more public ownership—Federal, State, and local—much the larger part of the forest land, and particularly of the productive capacity, will remain in private ownership.

The recommendations that follow refer especially to the Federal aspects of a long-range program, though cooperative action is often involved. Admittedly, they do not fully compass all unsatisfactory features of the present situation; for example, the 75 million acres of forest land which is wholly deforested or has so little restocking as to justify the description "idle." Nor do they adequately reach the additional millions of acres of run-down forests in small properties that need considerable

capital expenditure with long deferment of income.

To spell out the Federal phases of a long-range program does not minimize the opportunity and need for private or State action. In fact, strengthening of State forestry agencies is an important corollary of the Federal program. Much of this program aims to help private owners take care of their own lands; but private owners cannot reasonably be expected to do alone a job for which they are as yet unprepared and unequipped.

This program is aimed primarily at meeting American requirements for timber supply; but it should go far toward preventing soil erosion and safeguarding range forage, watershed, recreational, and other values which in some regions surpass that of the timber. If fully effective, it would provide a framework within which the short-range and many necessary detailed and supplemental measures could be worked out. It may be divided into three broad categories:

FIRST, a series of public aids to private forest landowners, especially the small owners. Some of these require new legislation. Others are already in effect but need strengthening.

SECOND, public control of cutting and other forest practices on private land sufficient to stop forest destruction and keep the land reasonably productive.

THIRD, expansion and intensified management of national, State, and community forests.

The principal measures embraced by the foregoing three categories follow.

I. Public Aids and Services to Private Owners

1. *Technical assistance to private owners in establishing and tending forests, and in harvesting and marketing forest products, should be made available on a broader and much larger scale than at present. Corresponding assistance should also be made available to operators of processing plants. The emphasis here is on owners of small properties and plants.*

The value of on-the-ground technical assistance and guidance to individual private owners of small properties has been impressively demonstrated by the present small program of the Forest Service in cooperation with State forestry agencies under the Norris-Doxey Act. Embracing some 650 counties in 40 States in the fiscal year 1948, 173 farm woodland management projects, each with a resident forester, were reaching only a small part of the farm-forest owners who desire such aid, even within the counties served. The Federal contribution to

ation by forest landowners and mill men as to the opportunities and advantages of sound forestry and processing methods. Forest extension is needed also to give the public, including farm youth, an understanding of the place of forest conservation in the economy of the Nation.

The Federal and State agricultural extension services have a key position in this educational work. At present these agencies in 45 States and 2 territories employ only 65 extension foresters. The Federal appropriation for fiscal year 1948 of $106,343 for this work was more than matched by the States. Other agencies of the Department of Agriculture also participate in some aspects of such work. Much good work is being done by private agencies. There is strong need for stepping up such activity by all agencies concerned.

3. Forest planting on private forest land should be greatly accelerated.

This measure is directed mainly to the problem of the 62 million acres of private forest land either denuded or so poorly stocked as to be practically idle, and to the additional millions of acres that should be converted to forest use. With adequate protection some will stock naturally, but a very large proportion should be planted.

Prior to 1947 only about 2½ million acres of private land had been successfully planted. In 1947 about 114,000 acres were planted.

Forest planting—the procurement of planting stock and its actual planting—is expensive. Except for some large owners and a few cooperative ventures, private forest planting has been almost wholly contingent upon getting planting stock from the States at a nominal price. Making stock available at, say, half of the actual cost to produce has proved a powerful stimulant, particularly as many small owners use their own labor in planting. The demand for planting stock under such terms far exceeds the supply.

The Federal Government participates in a small way financially insofar as the program applies to farmer landowners under the authority of Section 4 of the Clarke-McNary Act and the Norris-Doxey Act. This program is supplemented by other public and private agencies and particularly by the Soil Conservation Service in erosion control and in shelter-belt planting in the Prairie-Plains States. The work of all agencies needs to be greatly accelerated.

McNary Act to include nonfarm owners, who account for more than half of the private acreage, and by accelerating the Federal aid.

4. *A federally sponsored forest credit system should be established to make long-term loans on terms and conditions suitable for forestry purposes. Such credit should be adapted to the needs of private forest operators and made contingent upon sound forest practices.*

Forestry is the only major form of land use for which suitable credit facilities are not available. Although currently the demand for forest credit seems rather limited, the Forest Service believes that in the long run a system of forest credit adapted to the long-term nature of forestry would be an important aid to forest conservation. Such forest credit is needed, for example, to enable owners to consolidate holdings for more efficient management and protection; to facilitate stand improvement; to provide forest administrative, protection, and utilization facilities under sustained-yield management; to enable owners of young timber to pay carrying costs and thus prevent sacrifice of immature or economically unripe timber; and to refund unduly burdensome loans.

Most loans from private sources have been for fairly short terms and predicated on the liquidation of timber without regard to forestry considerations. By contrast, the capital required for the forestry purposes outlined above should be made available at relatively low cost and for sufficient periods to enable repayment in part from deferred timber yields. Only by Federal action can a forest credit system be established that will meet these requirements.

Such a system of forest credit should be established within the farm credit system through a forest credit bank or other arrangement to assure needed autonomy and responsibility for this field of credit. New legislation is needed to facilitate this measure.

Further study should be given to the practicability of a system of more liberal credit in connection with the rehabilitation of small, badly run-down properties which require considerable capital expenditure with long deferment of income.

5. *Provision should be made for a federally sponsored insurance system to reduce the risks inherent in forestry enterprises. Insurance agreements should require that insured property be managed under good forestry principles.*

Losses from fire and other destructive agents accost. The program is deficient in two important respects:

(a) Protection had not been established (in 1946) on 120 million acres. [2] It was in effect on 319 million acres. During that calendar year approximately 15 percent of the unprotected area burned as compared with less than 1 percent of the area under protection. Seventy percent of the unprotected area was in the South, one of our most important forest regions.

(b) With the exception of a few States, and portions of others, the protection needs to be intensified where it is already established.

The present annual Federal authorization of 9 million dollars is based on the estimate of 18¾ million dollars as the 1938 cost of adequate protection. For 1948 the corresponding cost would be more than double. This increase is due to the decreased purchasing power of the dollar, the higher cost of personal service attributable to other factors, an increase in the acreage in need of protection, and higher standards of adequate protection.

9. *Cooperative protection against forest insects and diseases should be strengthened by providing for more prompt and adequate action to discover and suppress incipient epidemics and control those which "escape."*

Chestnut, one of the most valuable hardwoods, was wiped out by blight. Blister rust, a foreign invader, threatens the valuable white and sugar pines. During the 20-year period ending in 1940, the western pine beetle destroyed, in California, Oregon, and Washington, approximately 25 billion board feet of ponderosa pine, having a stumpage value of approximately $100,000,000. The 1943–47 outbreak of the spruce bark beetle in Colorado killed more than 4 billion board feet of spruce, with a stumpage value of possibly $12,000,000. Many other illustrations could also be given which indicate that in the aggregate timber losses from forest pests exceed those from fire.

The Forest Service carries out control measures within the national forests and against losses threatening them. Other Federal agencies carry out control work with respect to land under their jurisdiction, largely on the basis of technical information assembled by the Bureau of Entomology and Plant Quarantine. Direct cooperative action without respect to ownership has been taken by the Bureau of Entomology and Plant Quarantine under

---

[2] In 1947 this was reduced to 111 million acres.

special authorization by Congress against three introduced pests.

Sound silvicultural practice is of itself a means of control. However, as in the case of fire, there is a need and public responsibility for organized detection and for control. The Forest Pest Control Act affords a legislative foundation for the needed development of such protection. This act declares the Federal responsibility in the control of forest insects and diseases on a Nation-wide basis and on lands in all classes of ownership; it gives the Secretary of Agriculture authority, as a condition of Federal cooperation in forest pest control, to require cooperation from the States or other public or private agency as he deems appropriate; and to authorize the establishment of adequate services and facilities for the detection of incipient outbreaks and their prompt suppression.

10. *All phases of forest research should be strengthened and expanded as a basic means of aiding forestry and improving wood utilization.*

Fundamental to the practice of forestry and to rapid progress in forest conservation is adequate knowledge of the techniques of forestry, and a thorough understanding of the benefits from proper use of timber, range, wildlife, recreation, and watershed resources. Because forest conditions and their economic relations to society are highly varied and complex, well-organized comprehensive research is essential to attain quickly and economically the goal of good forest management and use. The Federal Government, through the Department of Agriculture, has appropriately taken the lead in such research. The work, under authority of the McSweeney-McNary Act, is conducted mainly through the Forest Products Laboratory—a national institution—and 12 regional Forest and Range Experiment Stations, with a larger number of decentralized and strategically located experimental forests and ranges.

In expanding forest research programs of the Department of Agriculture and of other public and private agencies, special, but not exclusive, attention should be given to:

(a) Research in wood utilization to find means of reducing the enormous current waste of timber in the woods and mills, to find ways of utilizing the low-grade trees that now occupy valuable forest growing space, to improve the use of wood, and to develop new wood products and markets, including pilot plants to encourage the commercial application of new processes.

(b) Development of profitable methods for growing, protecting, and harvesting forest crops so as to build up the Nation's forest capital, increase yields of the more valuable tree species, and enable farmers and other owners to realize potential incomes from timber crops.

(c) Rapid completion and maintenance of the Forest Survey on standards that will provide basic resource data for sound public policies and private forest plans. Other economic studies are needed to remove some of the financial obstacles to improved forest management and utilization, to determine potential timber requirements, supplies, and markets, and to enable the United States to keep abreast of forest problems in other parts of the world which may affect the timber supply and forest-products industries of this country.

(d) Critical problems of range depletion and inadequate forage production on millions of acres of western ranges. Their solution requires research to find feasible methods for improving range management and for correlating range, wildlife, and watershed uses.

(e) Problems of water supply, erosion, and flood damage which require development of effective upstream flood control measures and efficient methods of managing watershed forests and other vegetation.

II. Public Control of Cutting and Other Forest Practices on Private Forest Lands

1. *A system of public regulation of cutting and other forest practices should be established that will stop forest destruction and keep forest lands reasonably productive. The States should continue to have opportunity to enact and administer adequate regulatory laws. However, in order to assure a consistent pattern—Nation-wide and in a reasonable time—a basic Federal law is needed.*

This basic legislation should establish standards as a guide for local forest practices and authorize Federal financial assistance to States which enact and administer regulatory laws consistent with the Federal requirements. It should also provide for Federal administration in States which request it or which, after a reasonable period, fail to put such regulation into effect.

The measures of public aid to private owners outlined in the preceding section are comprehensive and far-reaching. They will require substantial Federal expenditure and are justified by the

acres, of which 73.5 million is commercial forest land. Commercial forest land in other Federal ownership amounts to 15.4 million acres and State and local governments have 27.1 million acres.

Acquisition commenced in 1911 under the authority of the Weeks Law. About 18 million acres have been purchased—more than half during the emergency unemployment program between 1934 and 1937—and about 4 million acres have been acquired through exchange. Except for an appropriation of $3,000,000 for the fiscal year 1947, acquisition has been practically at a standstill since the outbreak of World War II.

Related to acquisition is the need for legislation that will remove inequities that exist in certain localities under the present system of financial contributions to local government on account of national forests, and also make these contributions more stable. The Forest Service favors a plan that will provide for an annual payment of an equitable percentage of the fair value of the forest property, probably three-fourths of 1 percent.

2. *Development and intensified management of the national forests should be vigorously pushed.*

These forests can contribute increasingly to our immediate and long-run needs for timber and other services. The following aspects are of high priority.

The first is more intensive timber management, to help meet the Nation's need for lumber and other forest products and to sustain local industries and communities. The rate of cutting has more than doubled since 1940 and is now about 4 billion feet annually. This can be increased considerably more. Many miles of new access-road construction are required. There is need, through sales and otherwise, to step up thinnings and other timber-stand-improvement cutting. Some 3¼ million acres of partly or wholly denuded national-forest land should be planted within the next 15 years. Vigorous efforts to establish a pulp and paper industry in Alaska, based on national-forest timber, should be continued.

Second, certain unsatisfactory range situations should be cleared up. National-forest range, of vital importance in watershed protection, never fully recovered from its severe exploitation during World War I despite sizable reductions in livestock numbers and other remedial measures. This calls for further downward adjustments in stocking on some allotments, along with improved management, the construction of range facilities, a large amount of range reseeding, and in some localities, a reduction of big-game population.

A third aspect is safeguarding and improving watershed values. Closer attention to this in all phases of management, a vigorous amplification of upstream flood and erosion control measures, and acceleration of watershed surveys authorized in the 1944 Flood Control Act, will go far toward attaining this objective.

Fourth is national-forest recreation. Recreational use of the national forests has greatly increased, and this upward trend is likely to continue indefinitely. Facilities are inadequate. Needed is a large amount of too-long-delayed maintenance, together with expansion of existing improvements.

Fifth is a considerably stepped-up program of wildlife management. The aim, on the one hand, should be to increase and stabilize the yield of the wildlife resources in recognition of the great public demand for good hunting and fishing; on the other, to avoid overstocking. Especially important in the long run are measures to maintain and improve wildlife habitat.

Sixth is intensified fire protection mainly through more effective fire prevention, establishment of a well-trained standby force, greater mechanization of fire fighting, and more use of aircraft. Similarly, protection against forest insects and diseases should be strengthened by better provision for detecting impending epidemics and for prompt control.

The expansion of forest research covered earlier in this section would be of large benefit in the development and intensified management of the national forests.

National-forest development and management are based on organic legislation which, generally speaking, is adequate. However, experience has revealed a number of points on which new legislation is needed to facilitate good administration. These were embodied in H. R. 2028 (80th Cong.).

The needed action outlined in the preceding pages is directed toward making the timber resources of the United States contribute their full potential to a prosperous national economy. Commensurate with this country's growing responsibility in world affairs, the Forest Service also recognizes the need to encourage international cooperation in forestry. For example, it aims to give all possible assistance in the forestry work of the United Nations Food and Agriculture Organization. It also will continue to work with the Pan American Union on inter-American forestry matters, and to supply information and advice to other countries seeking to improve their forests.

The time is already late. If the action outlined, and the efforts of all public and private forest landowners and agencies, were immediately effective in full, it would still require many years to achieve the proposed goals. The farther depletion and deterioration extend, the more difficult and costly the job of adequate forest restoration. The situation calls for broad-gage and farsighted action.

Forest Land and Its Uses

For three centuries the American people have been hewing an empire from a heavily wooded land. Both the amount of standing timber and the forest area have been reduced. But two-thirds of the original forest land remains, which is plenty, *if properly used,* eventually to furnish again all the forest wealth that a prosperous Nation needs.

This remaining forest land—624 million acres—adds up to one-third of the continental United States, exclusive of Alaska. This is as big an area as all the States east of the Mississippi River with Kansas and Louisiana thrown in. Forest acreage exceeds the total farm cropland by nearly one-fifth (fig. 1). It is larger than that of the open lands used for pasturage and range.

Mostly today's forest land is that which has escaped the plow: forest land undeveloped for other uses because of roughness, stoniness, poor soils, aridity, short growing season, or other unfavorable circumstances. It also includes worn-out or low-grade land that at one time or another has been farmed.

The great shrinkage in forest land that began with early settlement is largely the result of clearing for crops and pasture. The major competitor of forestry for use of land has always been crop agriculture, and therefore most of the reduction in forest acreage has been in the humid agricultural territory east of the Plains.

The total forest-land acreage probably will not change much from the present 624 million. It may even increase. Urban developments, and construction of highways and other facilities, are not likely to make significant reductions. Some of the better-grade lands, particularly in the East and on the Pacific Coast, will be cleared for agriculture. On the other hand, many millions of acres of the poorer cropland doubtless will revert to forest use.

Both the contributions and the problems of forestry are influenced by the close ties between forest and other agricultural land. Woodland is an integral economic feature of 3¼ million farms. Hundreds of thousands of farms are intermingled with nonfarm forest land. Thousands of farmers depend in whole or in part upon forest range for feeding their stock, and on forests for water supplies and other services. Many farmers earn cash in woods work. Moreover, forests help sustain industries and communities that provide the farmer with local markets for food, fiber, and livestock products.

America's forest lands are a vast domain of widely varying character and productiveness. From tidewater to timber line they include a rich variety of forest types and conditions. They are an important factor in the economy of every region except the Plains (fig. 2). East of the Plains they represent nearly half of all the land—about one-fourth of the Central region, 45 percent of the Lake, and half or more of the Middle Atlantic, the South, and New England. In the West they bulk largest in the Pacific Northwest, with more than half the area. The far-flung distribution and great variety of forest lands assure a wide sharing of their benefits and services.

In studies of timber resources forest land is usually divided into two broad categories. About three-fourths, 461 million acres, is classed as commercial because it is suitable and available for growing merchantable timber (table 1). The better and more accessible forest sites are of course in this class. The less-favored one-fourth, 163 million acres, is called noncommercial. It includes, for example, the open-grown mesquite and pinyon-juniper of the Southwest, the chaparral woodland in southern California, high alpine forests, and the oak-cedar breaks of Texas and Oklahoma. It also includes 13 million acres of better sites set apart for parks and game preserves.

Although forest land is chiefly thought of as a source of timber, both commercial and noncommercial forest land is valuable for watershed protection, for forage crops, for wildlife habitat, and for recreation. These values, essential to our economy and way of life, in some regions outweigh that of timber supply. Most of the forest land may be

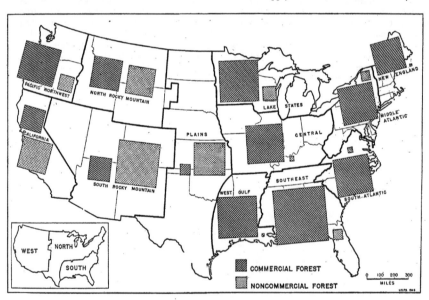

FIGURE 2.—Distribution of the forest lands of the United States by regions.

used effectively for more than one or for all of these purposes at the same time. In some areas, however, natural or economic conditions or critical situations call for restriction or exclusion of certain uses. Everywhere some correlation and adjustment are necessary to assure optimum benefits. This harmonizing of uses typifies forestry that adequately serves the public interest.

TABLE 1.—*Distribution of forest land of the United States, by section and region, 1945*

Section and region	Total forest land	Commer- cial	Non- commer- cial
North:	*Million acres*	*Million acres*	*Million acres*
New England	31.1	30.9	0.2
Middle Atlantic	44.2	41.6	2.6
Lake	55.7	50.3	5.4
Central	44.9	44.2	.7
Plains	35.8	3.3	32.5
Total	211.7	170.3	41.4
South:			
South Atlantic	43.8	42.9	.9
Southeast	91.9	89.4	2.5
West Gulf	51.1	50.9	.2
Total	186.8	183.2	3.6
West:			
Pacific Northwest	53.9	46.2	7.7
California	45.5	16.4	29.1
North Rocky Mtn.	53.2	29.1	24.1
South Rocky Mtn.	72.7	15.8	56.9
Total	225.3	107.5	117.8
United States	623.8	461.0	162.8

The major aspects of multiple use may be briefly described as follows:

1. *Watershed protection.*—An essential function of forests is to safeguard watersheds and their dependent water supply, power, and navigation facilities. Forest cover helps to regulate stream flow and minimize floods. It also keeps priceless soil in place and out of streams, reservoirs, and harbors.

The forest lands of the United States are well situated for watershed protection. About three-fifths of them are in the humid area east of the Plains. Here they are widely distributed, although the heaviest concentrations are in hilly or mountainous sections embracing the headwaters of most of the major streams. In the West the wooded slopes of high mountains and plateaus receive several times more rain and snow than the inhabited valley lands. These remote forest highlands therefore supply virtually all the ground water which

feeds perennial streams. Without them the valleys, and indeed most of the West, would be an arid waste.

At least three-fourths of the forest acreage has a major or moderate watershed influence, although misuse has greatly lessened the protective value of much of it. The other one-fourth—of minor influence—includes deep sands, swamps, and overflow areas, and other lands of mild topography such as occurs in the Lake States and coastal areas.

2. *Grazing.*—Forest lands furnish seasonal or year-round grazing for millions of domestic animals, which supply a substantial part of the Nation's meat, wool, and leather. With proper management most of the forest range can be grazed profitably and in harmony with other uses. Unregulated grazing, on the other hand, destroys the forage and seriously impairs other forest values as well.

More than half the forest land—about 350 million acres—is used for range. About 155 million acres of this is west of the Plains, where it represents nearly 70 percent of the forest land. An additional 142 million acres is in the South, chiefly in the piney woods and mountain sections. Some 53 million acres is in the North, mainly hardwood forests on farms, where grazing is undesirable.

3. *Forest recreation.*—Forest lands—widely used for camping, hunting, fishing, and other outdoor sports—afford a much-sought environment for enjoyment of nature and the esthetic. For many people, forests have inspirational and health-giving qualities that serve as antidote to the tensions of this fast-moving age.

Many million people seek some form of forest recreation each year. The demand is strongly upward. This continues a long-time trend—only temporarily halted by the war—which modern transportation, increased leisure, and other factors have greatly accentuated. The forests are under great pressure to meet recreation needs.

Most forest land has value for recreation. However, the usable territory is limited to about 400 million acres. Reasons for this, among others, are that the land is not accessible or its use for recreation is hampered by ownership or management policies. Except for hunting and fishing, most forest recreation is concentrated on the relatively small acreage that is reserved for scenic and recreational purposes.

4. *Wildlife production.*—Much of our rich wildlife heritage—fish, furbearing animals, bird life, and big game—is closely identified with forest rec-

reation and with forests. Virtually all forest land supports some wildlife. It is one of the most valuable products on a great deal of that classed as noncommercial.

Properly managed, the wildlife resource seldom interferes with other forest uses; but in some instances grazing and timber-cutting practices require modification to assure wildlife food and habitats. Additional forest land should be reserved primarily as game refuges to provide sanctuary and to restock surrounding territory. However, in aggregate, these reserves would include only a very small part of the total forest land.

5. *Timber supply.*—It is to the 461 million acres of commercial forest land that America must look for timber products. Three-fourths of this is in the populous North and the South (table 1). The West, with 40 percent of the total land area, has only 23 percent of the commercial forest land. Not all of it can yet be worked economically.

In the three southern regions and the Douglas-fir subregion of the Pacific Northwest climate and other factors are especially favorable for renewal and rapid growth of forests. These regions have 45 percent of the commercial forest land.

Seventy-five percent of the commercial forest land, generally including the more productive and accessible, is privately owned (table 2). Thirty percent, 139 million acres, is in farms;[4] nonfarm ownership accounts for 206 million acres, of which about 51 million are held by the basic wood-using industries—lumber and pulp companies.

Only a small part of private land is in medium and large holdings of 5,000 acres or more; the greater part is in small holdings—261 million acres in some 4¼ million properties, which average only 62 acres. These small holdings predominate in all the major sections of the United States (table 3), and from them stem many of the problems in American forestry.

Private holdings furnish about 90 percent of the timber cut. They will continue to be our main source of timber, although the relative contribution of public lands, particularly the national forests, is increasing.

Publicly owned commercial land makes up only one-fourth of the total. Federal agencies administer 89 million acres of this land; State and local governments, 27 million (table 2). National forests are the major Federal category, with about 73 million acres, chiefly in the West. National-forest land, for the most part, is in rough, often remote back country. Much of it, bearing old-growth timber, still awaits development. The bulk of the other Federal lands are in Indian reservations, the public domain and grazing districts, and in Oregon and California revested lands.[5]

Timber growing will always be a major function of commercial forest land. Today, timber needs are in the spotlight. The Nation needs ample, dependable wood supplies in its bid for peacetime prosperity. The outlook, now and in the years ahead, depend greatly on the condition of the timber growing stock—how it is handled and improved. The forest land is ample—the challenge lies in its management.

TABLE 2.—*Ownership of commercial forest land, 1945*

Ownership class	United States	North	South	West
	Million acres	Million acres	Million acres	Million acres
Private:				
Farm	139.0	61.0	69.0	9.0
Industrial and other	206.0	78.6	98.0	29.4
Total	345.0	139.6	167.0	38.4
Public:				
National forest	73.5	9.5	10.1	53.9
Other Federal	15.4	1.8	3.9	9.7
State and local	27.1	19.4	2.1	5.6
Total	116.0	30.7	16.1	69.2
All owners	461.0	170.3	183.1	107.6

TABLE 3.—*Distribution of private commercial forest land, by size of holding, 1945*

Section	All holdings	Small [1]	Medium [2]	Large [3]
	Million acres	Million acres	Million acres	Million acres
North	140	118	6	16
South	167	122	22	23
West	38	21	5	12
United States	345	261	33	51

[1] Less than 5,000 acres.
[2] 5,000 to 50,000 acres.
[3] Over 50,000 acres.

[4] This estimate was derived from the 1935 census. The 1945 census was not available when reappraisal data were compiled. Estimates of farm woodland may vary widely depending upon how "farm" is defined.

[5] The last-named, some 2 million acres of high-quality timberlands in western Oregon, are of more importance than their relatively small acreage would imply.

Timber Is a Crop

When white men began to settle this country the timber stand probably amounted to at least 8,000 billion board feet. This enormous volume was very largely in virgin timber, centuries old. Now we have about 1,600 billion board feet, only about half virgin. In the course of 300 years, and chiefly during the last century, we have used or destroyed most of our original timber heritage plus much of what has grown in the meantime. The time is long past when timber could safely be viewed as a reserve to be drawn upon without regard for replacement. It must now be regarded as a crop.

The timber crop must be harvested in trees of a size and quality suitable for commercial use;[6] and since about 80 percent of all timber products are cut from trees of saw-timber size, it is important to think of the timber crop primarily in terms of saw timber.[7]

To maintain an annual crop of merchantable timber, there must be a succession of age classes from seedlings up to full-grown timber so that as merchantable trees are cut each year new ones will be ready to take their places. If the age classes were properly balanced and the amount cut each year were equal to the annual growth, the

---

[6] Viewing commercial requirements in the broadest sense, trees 5 inches in diameter breast high or larger may be considered merchantable. Even for fuel wood, distillation wood, and other bulk products, it is not profitable to cut trees smaller than that. But for lumber the trees must be larger.

[7] Saw timber refers to trees large enough for sawlogs in accordance with practice of the region, regardless of actual use. Throughout the East softwood saw timber does not

volume of standing timber would remain constant. It could then be viewed as growing stock or forest capital on which the annual crop accrues as interest. In this light, until the productive capacity of the land is reached, the more growing stock or standing timber there is, the greater the crop available for cutting each year.

This does not apply strictly to virgin forests, because in them death and decay usually offset current growth. They do not fully meet the growing-stock concept until they have been converted to a net growing condition by removal of overmature trees.

The Timber Stand

As of the beginning of 1945, the stand of saw timber was estimated at 1,601 billion board feet (table 4 and fig. 3). The volume of all timber 5 inches or more in diameter breast high was 470 billion cubic feet. These are large figures. But critical examination shows that growing stock or forest capital is by no means satisfactory.

For one thing, growing stock east of the Great Plains is badly depleted. The land is generally understocked. Although three-fourths of the commercial forest land is in the East, the timber there —558 billion board feet—is little more than one-third of the national total (fig. 4). Largely second growth, it is generally of poorer quality than the virgin timber. Saw-timber stands in the North average only 3.8 thousand board feet per acre and in the South 3.3 thousand.

On the other hand, two western regions—the Pacific Northwest and California—with less than one-seventh of the commercial forest land, have more than half the saw timber in the United States. In

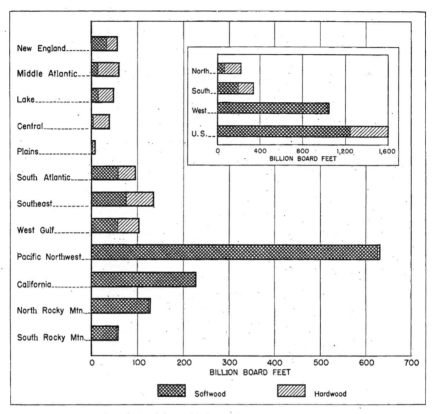

FIGURE 3.—Saw-timber stand in the United States, by region, 1945.

of saw timber in the West is in virgin stands. If these stands are cut so as to put them in good growing condition, the average volume needed as growing stock for future crops will generally be less than at present. Nevertheless, this backlog of forest capital is an extremely important part of our timber supply and should be carefully husbanded.

The occurrence of different species in different parts of the country is another basic element in the situation. Timber in the West is almost all softwood, the kind that is in greatest demand for the major industrial uses. But in the North about three-fourths is hardwood. Maine is the only northern State with more softwood than hardwood. Even in the South 43 percent of the saw timber is hardwood.

Half the saw timber in the United States is of three species (fig. 5):

Species:	Billion bd. ft.
Douglas-fir	430.0
Southern yellow pine [1]	188.3
Ponderosa pine	185.4
	803.7

[1] All commercial southern pine species grouped together.

18

TABLE 4.—*Timber volume, United States, 1945*

Section and region	Saw timber [1]			All timber [2]		
	Total	Soft-wood	Hard-wood	Total	Soft wood	Hard wood
	Billion bd ft.	*Billion bd ft.*	*Billion bd ft.*	*Billion cu. ft.*	*Billion cu. ft.*	*Billion cu. ft.*
North:						
New England	58	33	25	25	12	13
Middle Atlantic	62	14	48	27	5	22
Lake	50	15	35	23	7	16
Central	44	3	41	21	1	20
Plains	6	1	5	4	(*)	4
Total	220	66	154	100	25	75
South:						
South Atlantic	97	59	38	36	17	19
Southeast	136	77	59	54	24	30
West Gulf	105	58	47	41	18	23
Total	338	194	144	131	59	72
West:						
Pacific Northwest:						
Douglas-fir subregion	505	501	4	117	115	2
Pine subregion	126	126	(*)	29	29	(*)
Total	631	627	4	146	144	2
California	228	228	....	45	45	....
North Rocky Mtn.	127	126	1	33	33	(*)
South Rocky Mtn.	57	56	1	15	14	1
Total	1,043	1,037	6	239	236	3
United States	1,601	1,297	304	470	320	150

[1] "Saw timber" includes merchantable trees large enough to yield logs for lumber, whether or not they are used for this purpose. Because the minimum size of logs acceptable for lumber varies, the minimum size of saw-timber trees ranges from 9 to 23 inches d.b.h., depending upon the species and region.

[2] "All timber" includes trees 5 inches and larger in diameter breast high.

[3] Less than 0.5 billion.

There is now only 15 billion board feet of white and red pine, species that once were foremost in our lumber markets.

Oak is the leading hardwood, with 101 billion board feet, about equally divided between North and South. This is one-third of all the hardwoods. Birch, beech, and maple, as a group, come next with 68 billion board feet, mostly in the North.[8]

A most disturbing fact is that the forest growing stock continues to decline. The 1945 estimate of

[8] Additional details on species are given in: U. S. Forest Service. GAGING THE TIMBER RESOURCE OF THE UNITED STATES. (Reappraisal report 1.) Washington. 1946.

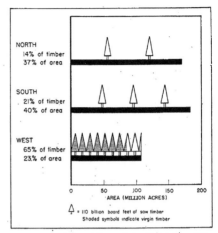

NORTH
14% of timber
37% of area

SOUTH
21% of timber
40% of area

WEST
65% of timber
23% of area

0   50   100   150   200
AREA (MILLION ACRES)

⌂ = 110 billion board feet of saw timber
Shaded symbols indicate virgin timber

FIGURE 4.—*Distribution of the saw timber, United States, 1945.*

1,601 billion board feet of saw timber is 43 percent less than reported by the Bureau of Corporations (Department of Commerce) for 1909, and 9 percent less than the Forest Service estimate for 1938.[9]

Although the 1938 and 1945 figures are not entirely comparable,[10] the fact of a major decline in saw-timber volume in recent years is clinched by figures for the regions where comparable data are available from the Forest Survey (table 5). The saw timber in 15 surveyed States dropped 156 bil-

[9] The decline since 1909 has probably been greater than indicated. The 1909 estimate did not fully recognize the smaller properties, and many species which are now merchantable were disregarded. Furthermore, in contrast to the practice 35 or 40 years ago, lumbermen and foresters now count trees of much smaller size as saw timber, particularly in the East.

[10] The 1938 estimates were weak in regions which have not been adequately surveyed. For example, more saw timber is now reported for the North than in 1938. The difference is primarily in the Middle Atlantic and Central States where hardwoods are reported at almost double the 1938 estimate. Such differences are much greater than could have resulted from growth even if there had been no cutting. They are partly due to an increase in the estimate of commercial forest acreage. In California also, where the progress of depletion is common knowledge, better estimates in 1945 resulted in a larger figure than in 1938. On the other hand, the 1945 estimates for the two Rocky Mountain regions are lower than in 1938 because a more realistic appraisal of operating prospects led to a reduction of almost 16 million acres in the commercial forest area.

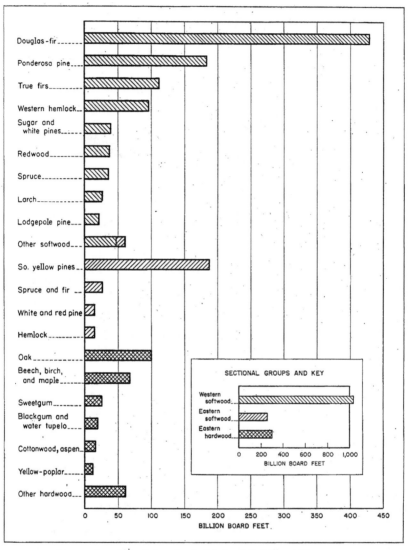

FIGURE 5.—Saw-timber volume, by kind of wood, United States, 1945.

TABLE 5.—*Decrease of saw-timber stand between original survey and 1945*

Region	Years of original survey	Decrease	
		Billion bd. ft.	*Percent*
Lake	1934–36	6.9	12
South Atlantic (N. C. and S. C. only)	1936–38	1.6	2
Southeast [1]	1932–36	22.0	15
West Gulf [2]	1934–36	13.0	12
Pacific Northwest [3] ...	1933–36	112.3	15
15 States.........	1932–38 [4]	155.8	14

[1] Tennessee not included.
[2] Northwestern Arkansas and northeastern Oklahoma not included.
[3] Volumes in original survey adjusted for subsequent shifts between commercial and noncommercial status.
[4] Median year, 1934.

lion board feet or 14 percent between the time of original survey and 1945—an average period of 11 years. These States contain 60 percent of the saw timber in the United States and account for about three-fourths of the annual cut.

Ownership of the Timber

Ownership is an important aspect of the timber situation because rate of cutting and measures taken to insure desirable new growth are related to the intent of the timber owner, and the stability of his tenure.

Up to the close of the last century the policy of this country was to turn the public domain over to private ownership in order to promote settlement and development. Not until practically all the land east of the Great Plains and much of the best and most accessible land of the West had passed into private ownership did concern for future timber supply lead to the setting aside of the national forests and a basic change in our policy of land disposal.

As a result of rapid exploitation of private timber and of a conservative policy in opening up the national forests—both related to economic circumstances—43 percent of the saw timber now stands on the 25 percent of the commercial forest land that is publicly owned (table 6 and fig. 6).

The proportion differs greatly between East and West. In the West almost one-half is in the na-

ownership; less than 40 percent is in private ownership. But the 397 billion board feet of western private timber, mostly in the Pacific Northwest and California, is generally more accessible and of better quality than the public timber.

TABLE 6.—*Ownership of saw timber, 1945*

Ownership class	North	South	West	United States
Public:	*Billion bd. ft.*	*Billion bd. ft.*	*Billion bd. ft.*	*Billion bd. ft.*
National forest	8	14	496	518
Other Federal.	2	4	98	104
State and local.	10	3	52	65
Total	20	21	646	687
Private:				
Farm	76	134	34	244
Other private...	124	183	363	670
Total	200	317	397	914
All owners...............	220	338	1,043	1,601

In the East, although the acreage in public ownership has been increased as a result of inability of private owners to hold and restore cut-over lands or of their willingness to sell, 93 percent of the saw-timber volume is privately owned. Clearly, public forests in the East are not able to make a very large contribution to national timber needs.

More than one-fourth of the private timber is on the farms. In the Central, Plains, and South Atlantic regions, farms contain more timber than do other private holdings. But in the Douglas-fir subregion of the Pacific Northwest, farms have only 4 percent of the private timber because most of the forest land on the farms is cut-over. The farm timber resources, especially in the East, contribute a good deal to the national timber supply. Properly managed, they can also be a more stable and better source of farm income.

Private timber in other than farm holdings is the major source of raw material for the timber industries at present. How much of the 670 billion board feet in this class of ownership is held by the industries themselves and how much is in the hands of other types of owners is not known. However, the lumber and pulp companies own only 15 percent of the private commercial forest land. Quite plainly, good management of the industrial timber holdings, although essential, will not of itself provide an adequate supply of timber prod-

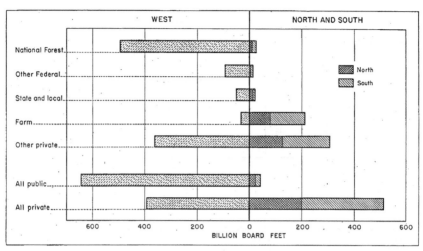

FIGURE 6.—*Ownership of saw timber in the United States, 1945.*

Growth Classes Not Well Balanced

It·is not enough to appraise forest growing stock in terms of its volume. The distribution of age classes and the quality are also important. Although age or growth classes should be balanced locally, it is only possible here to bring out major features of the situation for the North, South, and West (table 7).[11]

In the North almost half the commercial forest land bears only seedlings and saplings[12] or is denuded. Another one-fourth is in pole timber too small for sawlogs. Only 28 percent of the land bears stands of saw-timber size. A survey in New England showed that in 69 out of 118 mills, cutting primarily softwoods, the average log size was 10 inches or less. One may drive for miles through forest land in some parts of the North without seeing any merchantable saw timber.

In the South more than half the commercial forest land has been classified as saw timber; however, stands with only 600 board feet per acre. qualified as saw timber, in contrast with 2,000 board feet in most other eastern regions. Large

[11] For acreage by regions, see table 17 of reference given in footnote 8, p. 19.

[12] Trees up to 4 inches in diameter breast high.

saw timber is scarce in the South; stands with more than half the saw-timber trees over 18 inches in diameter occupy only 1 percent of the forest land. In the West Gulf and Southeast regions the average pine saw-timber tree is about 20 percent smaller than 10 years ago. An increasing number of mills are cutting 6-inch trees and it is not uncommon to see a logging truck carrying 50 or more logs. Obviously, mills operate on such small logs only because the supply of larger timber is scarce. In the Mississippi Delta many hardwood mills are operating on logs one-half or one-third as large as formerly

TABLE 7.—*Distribution of growth classes, in percent of commercial forest acreage, 1945*

Class of area	North	South	West	United States
Saw-timber:	*Percent*	*Percent*	*Percent*	*Percent*
Virgin	1.3	0.5	38.5	9.7
Second growth.	27.0	53.2	16.0	34.8
Total	28.3	53.7	54.5	44.5
Pole-timber	24.3	16.0	22.6	20.6
Seedling and sapling	29.0	12.5	12.4	18.6
Poorly stocked seedling and sapling, and denuded........	18.4	17.8	10.5	16.3
All areas........	100.0	100.0	100.0	100.0

Miscellaneous Publication 668, U. S. Department of Agriculture

In both North and South the keen demand for pulpwood, mine timbers, box-grade lumber, and other items which can be cut from small trees induces premature cutting of young trees which should be left to grow. This tends to perpetuate and aggravate the present shortage of larger timber.

In the West as a whole, virgin stands now occupy less than two-fifths of the commercial forest land, and one-fourth has been reduced to seedling and sapling growth or is denuded. Taking the Douglas-fir subregion of the Pacific Northwest alone, the latter proportion is even greater.

The 44.6 million acres of virgin forest contain more than half our saw-timber volume. But only one-fourth of this acreage meets the high standards popularly associated with virgin timber: heavy stands of large, high-quality trees of good species with little defect (table 8). The best of the virgin timber is in the Pacific Northwest. In California and the Rocky Mountain regions, which have half the acreage, half of it is rated as poor quality. For the country as a whole, 37 percent of the virgin forest is of poor quality. These poor-quality stands, containing only 15 percent of the total volume of virgin timber, are often very defective and of doubtful value. Some are long past their prime. Others contain a high percentage of inferior species; and others, now merchantable, are on poor sites which, as a practical matter, may never again grow good timber.

TABLE 8.—*Quality of virgin timber stands*

Region or section	Area	Stand quality		
		Good	Medium	Poor
	Million acres	Percent	Percent	Percent
Pacific Northwest	18.5	39	40	21
California and the Rocky Mountain regions	22.8	12	36	52
North	2.3	19	54	27
South	1.0	55	34	11
United States	44.6	25	38	37

Much of the Forest Land Is Poorly Stocked

Another indication that growing stock is below par is the prevalence of poor stocking—about 35 percent of all the commercial forest land is de-

	Poorly stocked and denuded forest land	
Section:	Million acres	Percent of commercial forest area
North	59.4	35
South	85.2	46
West	19.2	18
United States	163.8	35

This includes 58.0 million acres of second-growth saw timber; 30.5 million pole timber; and 75.3 million of seedlings, saplings, and denuded areas.

Almost nine-tenths of the poorly stocked stands are in the North and South. The southern forests are the most deficient, almost half being deforested or poorly stocked. In both North and South 35 to 40 percent of the second-growth saw timber and pole timber is poorly stocked and not over 25 percent is more than 70 percent stocked.

Of special significance is the 75.3 million acres of poorly stocked seedlings and saplings and wholly denuded lands. This idle forest land—representing about 1 acre in every 6—contributes little to the support of roads, schools, or other community services. It supports no jobs. Taxes, if paid, must come from other productive enterprise.

By and large, the rehabilitation of denuded forest land is a job that must be done by the public or with public aid if it is to be done. Yet 61.8 million acres or 82 percent of this idle land is in private ownership, as shown in the accompanying tabulation. Almost nine-tenths of this is in the East.

	Forest land		
Ownership:	All commercial (million acres)	Denuded [1] (million acres)	(percent)
Federal	89	7.1	8
State and local government	27	6.4	24
Private	345	61.8	18
All owners	461	75.3	16

[1] Includes poorly stocked seedling and sapling areas.

Only 8 percent of the commercial forest land in Federal ownership is denuded, or nearly so, in contrast to 24 percent for the forests held by State and local governments and 18 percent for the private lands. The Federal percent is low because these forests, largely in the West, have been protected for many years, and cutting on them has been generally good. The high percent for State and local public forests reflects the denuded condition in which so much of this land in the East came into public ownership, often through tax delinquency.

It is reasonable to assume that the acreage of

poorly stocked land will shrink as a result of improved fire protection and better cutting practices. Indeed, surveys in the South indicate that stocking in that region is better now than it was a decade ago. Young growth is springing up on millions of acres now protected from fire. This is one of the hopeful signs.

Quality of Timber Is Declining

Exploitation of the forests has lowered timber values in a number of ways. "High-grading"—cutting the best trees and leaving the poor—destructive cutting, and fire have all replaced valuable timber with inferior stands.

Evidence from all regions makes it clear that the fine logs needed by many forest industries are no longer abundant. This is serious because only after a long period of purposeful management can second growth approach the high quality of the original timber.

In the Northwest, the young and rapidly expanding Douglas-fir plywood industry faces major readjustment almost before it has hit its full stride. In the South, veneer manufacturers have difficulty maintaining an adequate flow of suitable hardwood logs. Some piece out their supply with logs from South America.

White oak suitable for tight cooperage is playing out also. Some operators are going after as few as 10 trees per 40 acres.

So it is with other items. The end of Port Orford cedar for battery separators is in sight. The cedar-pole industry faces radical curtailment. Hickory ski blanks are hard to get. Durable heart cypress in any quantity will soon be a thing of the past.

High-grading, as to both species and quality, began in Colonial days with the combing of the eastern seaboard for white pine masts and oak ship timbers. It went through another cycle as the country's growing lumber industry took the virgin white pine in the Middle Atlantic and New England States, leaving spruce and hardwoods for a later generation.

Before the pulp and paper industry became an important factor, lumbermen had again worked over the northeastern forests, selecting the big spruce that could be logged to the drivable streams. Pulp operations, in turn, have been concentrated on the remaining spruce and balsam fir, practically eliminating these species from some of the mixed stands and leaving much of the land in possession of hardwoods, which are often unmerchantable and highly defective.

Even where the northern hardwoods could be marketed, operators sought out the best yellow birch for veneers and sugar maple for flooring, furniture, etc. Beech, although an important species, has been largely neglected, not only because the wood is more difficult to season, but also because the trees are so commonly defective.

In southern New England the deterioration of the sprout hardwood forest by repeated cutting and fire (accentuated by the blight which killed all the chestnut some 25 to 30 years ago) has left little timber attractive to the timber industries. In fact, forest management here is handicapped by the difficulty of disposing of the inferior growth that now preempts so much of the land.

In the Middle Atlantic region between 5 and 6 million acres that once bore good commercial stands have been hit particularly hard. Destructive logging and repeated burning have almost desolated much of the oak-pine land of New Jersey. Similar practices in eastern Pennsylvania converted a large acreage of good forest to scrub oak. Under organized protection some of this land is slowly recovering, but the composition and quality of the new forest are distinctly inferior to what might have been maintained, as is shown by isolated tracts that escape destruction.

In the Lake region forest deterioration is an old story. It has perhaps been more complete and more extensive than in any other region and it is still continuing. Farm woodlands in the oak-hickory sections are mostly stocked with short, limby, and defective trees. Farther north, 5 million acres which once bore magnificent pines now grow scrubby aspen—scrubby because on that dry, sandy soil aspen grows slowly and deteriorates at an early age. This scrubby and often worthless timber greatly impedes the growth of conifer plantations. As for saw timber, since 1936 the volume of white pine and red pine has dropped 29 percent; birch, beech, and maple together have declined 16 percent; but the volume of the much less desirable aspen increased 55 percent.

During the war, Missouri produced only about 32 million board feet of softwood lumber a year. Yet in 1899 its softwood output was 273 million board feet. Although from 250 to 300 million board feet of hardwood lumber is still cut in the State, the forests of the Ozarks have largely degenerated into a stand of small and inferior timber

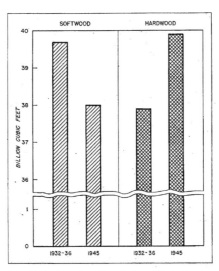

Figure 7.—*Southern pine volume declines while hardwoods gain. Data refer to total volume of all trees 5 inches and larger in 32 survey units containing 82 percent of all timber in the West Gulf and Southeast regions.*

Some of the Timber Is Not Operable

Although much timber not now merchantable may find a market as forest depletion and timber shortage become more acute, we cannot count on using all the timber included in the inventory. There will always be some timber beyond the economic pale. The volume may be less in periods of especially strong demand; and it may be more in periods of depression. It will not always be the same trees, or in the same stands.

Some inoperable timber lies in localities that have already been reached by commercial operations. This is inoperable in a more permanent sense than the timber in parts of the West that have not yet been opened up. Some of it is inoperable because it is so defective, scattered, in such small blocks, or in such difficult locations that it may never be economically feasible to get it out. For instance, 100 billion board feet of saw timber occurs in stands too light to justify commercial operation. The poor quality of some of the virgin stands has already been mentioned. Small size and limited utility of certain species may also keep some timber beyond economic access. In mixed stands, moreover, trees of inferior species or poor quality are often lost if they cannot be marketed along with the better trees.

Although the aggregate effect of these factors cannot be dependably estimated, it is important to make allowance for economic unavailability in calculating allowable cut or establishing growth goals.

Our Use of the Timber Resource

Shrinking Supply Limits Timber Use

The continued shrinkage and deterioration of forest growing stock is the heart of the Nation's forest problem. It means that we cannot use timber as generously as in the past. For example, the difficulty of getting lumber has driven lumber prices up more than those of other construction materials. Relief that may come from more rapid cutting of the present timber stand will at best be temporary or partial. The tide of depletion must be turned if the forests are to make their full contribution to the economic and social life of the Nation.

To help turn the tide every effort should, of course, be made to reduce waste in logging, manufacture, and use. Losses from fire, insects, disease, and other destructive agents should also be reduced. But above all, more timber should be grown—the extent of denuded land and the widespread occurrence of poor stocking and inferior quality indicate that much of the productive capacity of the land is going to waste. Good cutting practices in the virgin timber also offer opportunity for increasing timber growth. But saw timber cannot be grown overnight—and timber shortage is pressing us now. To bring the problem of timber use and depletion into focus, it is necessary to examine current growth and drain.[13]

Timber Growth

The forests of the United States are now growing at a yearly rate of 13.4 billion cubic feet of all timber including 35.3 billion board feet of saw timber[14] (table 9). Over half of the saw-timber growth (56 percent) is in the South. Only one-fourth is in the North, although the North has almost as much commercial forest land as the South. The remaining one-fifth is in the West.

In the eastern half of the country, where practically all the forest land has been cut over one or more times, current growth really measures the extent to which present practices utilize the productive capacity of the land. In the West, on the other hand, timber growth may be expected to increase as cutting progresses, because two-fifths of the commercial forest land is still in virgin timber, making little or no net growth. Effective saw-timber growth can be obtained promptly in some virgin forest types by selective cutting, which would take the overmature and decadent trees and leave a vigorous growing stock. Clear-cutting of a whole area, however, usually postpones effective saw-timber growth 50 years or more.

The current estimate of saw-timber growth is 3.3 billion board feet greater than the 1938 estimate. Most of the difference may be due to the nature of the estimates rather than to changes actually taking place. For example, earlier estimates were weaker and generally lower than current estimates in regions not reached by the Forest Survey, notably the New England, Middle Atlantic, Central, and California regions.[15] Such increases were partly offset by a reduction in the area of commercial forest land in the Rocky Mountain regions. An improved method of calculating growth led to an increase over the earlier estimate for the Douglas-fir subregion. Only for the Lake region and the South are the estimates comparable.

In the Lake region saw-timber growth dropped 24 percent in 10 years, with the decline more acute for softwoods than hardwoods. Total cubic-foot growth declined 17 percent.

In the South[16] saw-timber growth is 3 percent greater than it was 10 years ago. However, the net increase of 622 million board feet is the result of

---

[13] Timber drain measures the total volume removed from the forest by cutting (including waste and breakage in logging) and by losses from fire, wind, ice, epidemics of insects or disease, and other destructive agents. Endemic losses from insects and disease are accounted for in growth computations.

[14] See footnote 7, p. 17, for definition.

[15] See footnote 10, p. 19.

[16] These figures are based on the South as defined in the 1938 appraisal. Kentucky and West Virginia are included in addition to the three regions comprising the South in this report. Even here estimates are not fully comparable. Four States (Va., W. Va., Tenn., and Ky.) were not covered by the Forest Survey in 1938, and in 1945. Survey data were available for only one of these (Va.).

an increase of 886 million board feet (12 percent) of hardwoods and a decrease of 264 million board feet (2 percent) of softwoods. Similarly, two-thirds of a 9-percent increase in all-timber growth is in hardwood. Thus break-down of the growth figures confirms evidence in the previous section on the replacement of the more desirable pine by hardwoods. The over-all figures, which superficially indicate an improvement, really reflect deterioration of the forest.

TABLE 9.—*Current annual timber growth* [1]

Section and region	Saw-timber growth			All-timber growth		
	Total	Soft-wood	Hard-wood	Total	Soft-wood	Hard-wood
	Billion bd. ft.	*Billion bd. ft.*	*Billion bd. ft.*	*Billion cu. ft.*	*Billion cu. ft.*	*Billion cu. ft.*
North:						
New England	1.80	0.91	0.89	0.90	0.42	0.48
Middle Atlantic	2.71	.60	2.11	1.40	.27	1.13
Lake	1.40	.34	1.06	.81	.18	.63
Central	2.25	.13	2.12	1.44	.10	1.34
Plains	.19	.02	.17	.12	.01	.11
Total	8.35	2.00	6.35	4.67	.98	3.69
South:						
South Atlantic	6.11	4.02	2.09	1.76	1.01	.75
Southeast	8.22	5.28	2.94	2.71	1.48	1.23
West Gulf	5.61	3.62	1.99	1.92	1.03	.89
Total	19.94	12.92	7.02	6.39	3.52	2.87
West:						
Pacific Northwest:						
Douglas-fir sub-region	3.74	3.67	.07	1.02	.99	.03
Pine sub-region	.48	.48		.22	.22	
Total	4.22	4.15	.07	1.24	1.21	.03
California	1.16	1.16		.33	.33	
North. Rocky Mtn.	1.31	1.30	(²)	.54	.54	(²)
South Rocky Mtn.	.32	.32	(²)	.20	.18	.02
Total	7.01	6.93	.08	2.31	2.26	.05
United States	35.30	21.85	13.45	13.37	6.76	6.61

[1] Data for 1944.
[2] Less than 0.005.

Timber Drain

Forest drain, or the volume taken by cutting, and by fire and other destructive agents, was 13.7 billion cubic feet in 1944 (tabulation following). Of the all-timber drain, almost 80 percent, or the equivalent of 53.9 billion board feet, was saw timber. Hardwoods comprise 40 percent of the all-

timber drain, but less than 30 percent of the saw-timber drain.

	Forest drain	
	All timber [1] (billion cu. ft.)	Saw timber [2] (billion bd. ft.)
Timber cut, 1944	12.18	49.66
Fire losses [3]	.46	.86
Insect and disease losses [3]	.62	1.93
Windstorm and other losses [3]	.40	1.44
Total	13.66	53.89

[1] Excluding bark.
[2] Lumber tally.
[3] Average volume destroyed yearly in period 1934-43.

Although domestic use of wood was sharply reduced because of the war, saw-timber drain in 1944 was over 6 billion board feet more than in 1936, the year of the last previous comprehensive estimate. During the peak years 1941-43, saw timber drain was close to 60 billion board feet annually. It was again close to this figure in 1947.

About nine-tenths of the drain is due to cutting. The remainder is the work of fire, insects, diseases, and other natural causes. Not included in the drain figures is the loss by destructive agents of millions of small trees below 5 inches in diameter, which are no less important for future timber supply. Also serious are the deterioration of forest soil and the adverse watershed conditions resulting from fire and destructive cutting.

Nearly half the all-timber drain occurs in the South, which has only 28 percent of the Nation's timber, while about one-fourth each occurs in the North and West, with 21 and 51 percent of the timber, respectively (table 10).

Saw-timber drain from the South (25 billion board feet) is 25 percent greater than that from the West (20 billion board feet), even though the timber in the South is now almost all second growth and the West still has a large volume of virgin timber. Because of the advanced stage of depletion in the North, only 17 percent of the saw-timber drain now comes from that section, despite its great consumption of lumber. The rate of drain in relation to saw-timber volume is greater for softwoods than for hardwoods in both North and South.

Lumber is by far the largest item (table 11 and fig. 8), making up about 70 percent of the saw timber and 55 percent of the cubic-foot cutting drain. The lumber cut in 1944 was about 5 billion board feet more than in 1936 but 6 billion less than in 1929, and 5 billion less than in 1947. About three-fourths of the 34.4 billion board feet

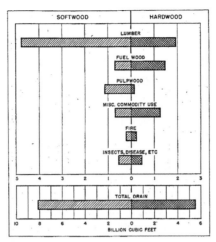

FIGURE 8.—*Annual forest drain by cutting (1944) and destructive agents (1934-43), United States.*

direct fuel-wood drain is from saw timber, and much of this is potentially more valuable for other products. It should not be necessary to cut much saw timber for fuel, or to clear-cut pole timber, if cutting for fuel were regarded as a tool of good forestry rather than the end point in timber harvest. Farmers, especially, could improve their stands by getting more fuel wood from thinnings, from trees of undesirable form or species, and from more complete utilization of trees cut for other purposes.

TABLE 11.—*Forest drain, by commodities cut, 1944*

TABLE 12.—*Major items of forest drain by region, 1944*

Section and region	Lumber		Fuel wood	Pulp-wood	Other commodities [1]	Fire [2]		Insects, disease, etc. [2]
	Million bd. ft.	*Million cu. ft.*	*Million cu. ft.*	*Million cu. ft.*	*Million cu. ft.*	*Million bd. ft.*	*Million cu. ft.*	*Million cu. ft.*
North: [1]								
New England	864	201	194	154	82	3	5	125
Middle Atlantic	1,361	313	224	52	204	23	18	35
Lake	1,170	333	96	179	90	8	6	43
Central	1,479	395	380	32	291	102	57	46
Plains	36	9	79	....	10	1	1	19
Total	4,910	1,251	973	417	677	137	87	268
South:								
South Atlantic	3,536	707	373	166	133	48	24	193
Southeast	6,867	1,356	498	257	473	229	149	289
West Gulf	3,819	774	298	152	398	156	107	113
Total	14,222	2,837	1,169	575	1,004	433	280	595
West:								
Pacific Northwest	10,877	1,934	36	309	232	131	44	63
California	2,496	372	2	....	22	91	29	65
North Rocky Mtn.	1,499	246	19	5	20	61	17	9
South Rocky Mtn.	387	71	4	....	7	6	3	19
Total	15,259	2,623	61	314	281	289	93	156
United States	34,391	6,711	2,203	1,306	1,962	859	460	1,019

[1] Veneer logs, hewn ties, mine timbers, fence posts, cooperage stock, shingles, and other small items.
[2] Average volume destroyed annually, 1934–43.

Pulpwood is a rapidly increasing element in drain (table 11 and fig. 8). In 1929 it totaled 4 percent of the commodity drain; in 1936, 6 percent; and in 1944, 11 percent. This increase has been largely due to the rapid expansion of the pulp and paper industry in the South. Remarkable advances in adapting the sulfate pulping process (using pine) to a wide variety of important commercial products, have led to the erection or enlargement of some 20 mills in the South since 1931 and additional units are under construction.

Pulpwood drain in the South now exceeds that of the North by nearly 40 percent. It exceeds that of the West by over 80 percent (table 12). In the Pacific Northwest, however, is concentrated some 309 million cubic feet, which is almost one-fourth the total for the country.

Nearly nine-tenths of the pulpwood cut in the South is pine. In the North, spruce, fir, hemlock, and pine make up three-fourths. Pulpwood in the West is chiefly spruce, true fir, and hemlock.

Although the specifications are more exacting than for fuel wood, more of the pulpwood also could be obtained from thinnings, improvement cuttings, and waste. As it is, however, all but a small fraction of the pulpwood cut is taken from the forest in harvest cuttings.

Other products.—Whereas lumber, fuel wood, and pulpwood make up 84 percent of the total commodity drain, the remaining 16 percent comprises more than 25 items including, in order of cubic volume cut annually, veneer logs, hewn ties, round mine timbers, fence posts, cooperage stock, and shingles. Although small in volume, poles for rural electric lines are an important item. The South accounts for more than half the drain in these miscellaneous items, the North one-third, and the West only one-seventh.

Comparison of Growth and Drain

Comparison of growth and drain is an instructive but often overworked criterion of the Nation's forest situation. Because of the great difference between regions as to forest conditions and stage of depletion, over-all figures may be misleading; and for the same reason regional figures should not be uniformly interpreted. Furthermore, it would be of little value to balance growth and drain by bringing timber use down to the present inadequate level of growth. To fully meet national needs and objectives, as will be shown in the next chapter, it will be necessary to balance growth against a level of consumption and drain higher than at present.

The near balance between all-timber drain (13.7 billion cubic feet) and all-timber growth (13.4 billion cubic feet) is deceptive (table 13). These figures mask the fact that for softwoods the drain is 21 percent more than growth, while for hardwoods it is 17 percent less. Furthermore, four-fifths of the drain is in saw timber. Saw-timber drain is more than 50 percent greater than saw-timber growth. The Nation should not be satisfied with a balance based on poles and saplings when its forest industries depend so largely on saw timber.

TABLE 13.—*Comparison of timber growth and drain, 1944*

Species group and section	Saw timber			All timber		
	Growth	Drain	Drain ratio [1]	Growth	Drain	Drain ratio [1]
All species:	*Billion bd. ft.*	*Billion bd. ft.*	*Percent*	*Billion cu. ft.*	*Billion cu. ft.*	*Percent*
North	8.4	9.0	108	4.7	3.7	79
South	19.9	24.9	125	6.4	6.5	101
West	7.0	20.0	285	2.3	3.5	152
United States	35.3	53.9	153	13.4	13.7	102
Softwood:						
North	2.0	3.0	150	1.0	1.0	96
South	12.9	15.6	121	3.5	3.7	105
West	6.9	19.9	287	2.3	3.5	155
United States	21.8	38.5	176	6.8	8.2	120
Hardwood:						
North	6.4	6.0	95	3.7	2.7	74
South	7.0	9.3	132	2.9	2.8	96
West	.1	.1	75	([2])	([2])	25
United States	13.5	15.4	114	6.6	5.5	83

[1] Computed before rounding data to tenths of billions.
[2] 0.05 or less.

In the West, drain is much greater than growth (fig. 9), but the virgin timber eases the situation there for the present. Nevertheless, hard times will come for dependent communities unless the virgin stands are cut at a rate and in a manner that will promote future growth. Without good forest practice and farsighted planning for both private and public lands, waning of the virgin timber may usher in a long period when there will not be enough saw timber to fully sustain the timber industries. This has already happened in some localities, notably around Puget Sound in western Washington and Klamath Falls in central Oregon.

In the North, saw-timber drain is only 7 percent more than saw-timber growth; drain for all timber is 21 percent less than growth. Yet the forest situation is more acute than in the other sections. Largely as a result of the advanced stage of forest

depletion and deterioration, many of the older wood-using plants have been forced out of business and the shortage of good timber makes it difficult for new plants to start. The excess of all-timber growth over drain is a reflection of the inferior quality and small size of a large part of the timber. Growth on timber of this character is a doubtful asset. In fact, one of the major forest problems of the North is to find markets for the small low-grade timber which should be gotten out of the way to make room for more valuable growth.

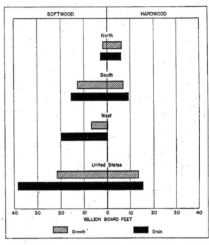

FIGURE 9.—*Annual growth and drain of saw timber, United States, 1944.*

In the South all-timber drain is not far out of balance, but saw timber—both hardwood and softwood—is being cut much faster than it is growing.

These trends, if continued, mean an increasing shortage of good timber and a serious handicap to the timber industries.

A Twenty-Year Projection

What has been happening to our saw-timber supply may be emphasized by theoretically projecting 1944 drain and cutting practices ahead for, say, 20 years. Actually, of course, the increasing difficulty of obtaining timber, especially in the North and South, makes it unlikely that the forest industries could produce for long at the 1944 rate.

Furthermore, an increasing number of private owners are practicing better forestry; and fire protection is becoming more effective. But if the 1944 cutting practices and rate of drain were continued regionally, the saw-timber stand would fall 27 percent in the next 20 years (table 14).

In this theoretical projection the Southeast region would suffer the biggest drop (60 percent), with the Pacific Northwest second (39 percent). Significantly, these are the Nation's principal timber-producing regions.

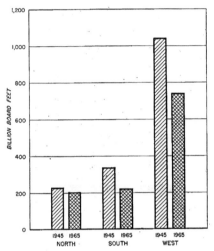

FIGURE 10.—*How saw-timber volume would change in 20 years, if 1944 drain and cutting practices were continued.*

For the South as a whole, a continuation of the 1944 cut and prevailing forest practices for 20 years would mean a decline of 117 billion board feet, or one-third of the present saw-timber volume (fig. 10). Obviously such a decline in saw-timber volume would mean curtailment of the forest industries and drastic readjustment in dependent communities. Such economic and social losses would be serious for the South, which needs additional industrial development to offset the displacement of labor by reduction of the acreage in cotton and by mechanization of its cultivation and harvesting.

In actual quantity, the greatest reduction of saw timber is taking place in the Douglas-fir subregion

where 20 years more at the 1944 rate would bring the volume down 206 billion board feet. Such a reduction, while not alarming statistically, would be accompanied by the closing of many established mills and continued shift of industrial activity from one locality to another.

Twenty years more of the present drain would not materially reduce the saw-timber stands in the rest of the country. However, depletion of ponderosa pine, western white pine, sugar pine, and redwood would force western forest industries to adapt themselves to the production and marketing of a different class of products.

If this 20-year projection were to become a reality, it would impair the chances for full employment, increase the burden of taxation on other forms of property, and affect our national security.

Though some adverse effects of timber depletion can hardly be avoided, the United States need not remain the victim of such circumstances. Our land resource is adequate; our people are making some progress in protecting and managing the forests for future timber crops. The time is ripe for more positive measures to make our forests more productive.

TABLE 14.—*Estimated effect of continuing 1944 drain and cutting practices for 20 years*

Section and region	Present stand	Prospective growing stock	Change
	Billion bd. ft.	*Billion bd. ft.*	*Percent*
North:			
New England	58	49	—16
Middle Atlantic	62	71	+14
Lake	50	35	—30
Central	44	43	— 2
Plains	6	6	....
Total	220	204	— 7
South:			
South Atlantic	97	93	— 4
Southeast	136	55	—60
West Gulf	105	73	—30
Total	338	221	—35
West:			
Pacific Northwest:			
Douglas-fir subregion	505	299	—41
Pine subregion	126	84	—33
Total	631	383	—39
California	228	187	—18
North Rocky Mtn.	127	119	— 6
South Rocky Mtn.	57	52	— 9
Total	1,043	741	—29
United States	1,601	1,166	—27

Miscellaneous Publication 668, U. S. Department of Agriculture

Sound Policy Calls for Abundant Growth

Forestry is a long-time undertaking. While the country's annual cut may vary somewhat with the play of economic forces, the rate of annual growth does not change appreciably from one year to the next. Once the forest resources have deteriorated as they now have done, it requires years of effort and additional investment to greatly increase the volume of cut that can be sustained. It is therefore important to set up long-range goals or objectives of forest growth as a basis and guide for sound public policy and action.

The Forest Service believes, on the basis of careful study, that the United States should aim to grow 18 to 20 billion cubic feet of timber annually, including 65 to 72 billion board feet of saw timber, which should be largely of good species and quality. These goals, as will be shown later, cannot be attained for several decades.

Obviously there must be a large element of judgment in formulating a reasonable objective when it involves looking many years into the future. The goal here proposed for saw timber is more than the 59.4 billion board feet of annual drain during the prosperous years 1925–29. But the whole economy is now running at a much higher level than in that period, and there is every reason why it should continue to do so. The goal likewise is more than the peak wartime drain which was also about 60 billion board feet. But during the war we were unable to keep abreast of the demand. Stocks of lumber were reduced to the vanishing point and civilian needs were largely neglected.

The proposed goals are formulated with the conviction that national well-being will continue to call for a larger output of goods and services than was ever known in peacetime. Natural resources will be a vital factor in such a high-level economy. There is no evident reason why this country should not take advantage of the potential productivity of its forest resource, one of the most important of all resources and one which, unlike minerals, is renewable.

The United States has been the greatest consumer of wood in the world. Wood is a basic, if not indispensable, element in the daily lives of our people. While some uses for wood decline, new uses are continually being found for it. The timber products industries are an important element in the support of many communities, both large and small. The Nation needs ample, dependable timber supplies to sustain and expand the supply of consumer goods and the industry and employment that are based on wood. Furthermore, as dramatically demonstrated by the recent war, an ample timber supply is a vital aspect of national security. Beyond these considerations is the world shortage of softwood timber. If its large potential forest yield were developed this country could safely help to meet world timber needs in years to come, and so contribute to international peace and well-being.

The proposed goals for timber growth take all of these potentialities into account.

Domestic Requirements

The principal element in the growth goal is timber for domestic use. How much this country will use in years to come will depend in large part upon available supply and economic conditions.

But it is not a function of this report to forecast economic conditions. As a sounder guide for public policy, this part of the growth goals is based on "potential requirements," which means the amount of timber a prosperous Nation might use if the supply were sufficient to keep forest products of suitable kind and quality available at reasonable prices.[17] Such requirements will almost certainly be higher than past consumption. Our population was much smaller in the years when the supply was still ample. Then for a decade consumption was held down by business depression. With wartime prosperity, output was hampered by shortage of men and equipment. And now one factor handicapping use is timber shortage. Prices of lumber have risen much faster than those of other construction materials,[18] and in 1947 were more than three times as high as in 1936.

To aim at less than potential requirements as defined here would be to sell America short.

In the aggregate, the estimate of potential requirements corresponds to an annual drain of 61 billion board feet from saw-timber trees:

Timber product:	Potential requirements (1950-55) in terms of annual drain	
	(billion cu. ft.)	(billion bd. ft.)
Lumber	8.7	44.3
Pulpwood	1.7	5.8
Fuel wood	1.8	3.1
Veneer logs and bolts	.6	2.8
All other	1.8	5.0
Total	14.6	61.0

Projecting these estimates several decades ahead results in some modifications of individual items but no significant change in total.

Lumber will continue to account for the bulk of timber use. Housing needs, unmet for the past 15 years, will constitute a heavy demand for lumber during the next 5 or 10 years at least. Today's shortage, precipitated by the return of servicemen to civilian life, has been in the making since the depression cut down normal construction in the early 1930's. In 1946 the National Housing Agency estimated that more than 3 million families lacked housing of their own and were "doubled up" with others. More than 7 million families, not including those on farms, were living in substandard

[17] In order to focus this analysis, primary estimates of potential requirements are based on the period 1950-55 with an assumed gross national product (in 1944 dollars) of $200 billion. Since the assumption of ample supply to keep prices of forest products (now badly out of balance) at reasonable levels could not be attained by 1955, the estimates have also been projected several decades ahead. Fuller discussion is given in Reappraisal Report 2, Potential Requirements for Timber Products in the United States. U. S. Dept. Agr. Forest Service. 1946.

[18] The Bureau of Labor Statistics index of wholesale lumber prices for December 1947 was 303 compared with 191 for all building materials, including lumber.

houses. A program to build 12½ million nonfarm residential units in the next 10 years was envisioned.[19] This is a high goal.

In addition to housing, the high level of industrial activity contemplated in potential requirements implies a larger volume of general construction than before the war. Construction of all sorts is an important feature of our industrial economy; it has sometimes been viewed as the balance wheel. An expanding volume of construction offsetting a trend toward use of proportionately less wood will tend to keep the demand for lumber high.

Similarly, a 200-billion-dollar economy will call for more lumber for shipping purposes than was used before the war. It will also mean a larger demand for lumber used in manufacture. An era of home building means a heavy demand for furniture. And the demand for many other manufactured articles tends to rise with consumers' spending power.

All together, under the assumed conditions of full employment and plentiful supply, potential lumber requirements a decade hence are placed at 44 billion board feet of timber as compared to 34 billion of lumber drain in 1944 and about 40 billion in 1947.

Looking farther ahead, estimated lumber requirements are somewhat less. For one thing, the trend toward smaller houses and less lumber per house, if continued, might more than offset the demand of a larger population for more dwelling units. But there is no reason for placing long-range lumber requirements at less than 40 billion board feet.

Pulpwood consumption has been expanding rapidly for 40 years. In recent years this has been due largely to increasing consumption of paper bags, cardboard boxes, and building boards. Consumption of paper and paperboard may reach 28 million tons in the next decade. This is the basis for an estimated requirement of 20 million cords of domestic pulpwood as compared with a cut of 15 million in 1944 and 17 million in 1946.

Long-range requirements, estimated from possible per-capita consumption with allowance for further improvement in manufacturing methods, are placed at 40 million cords of pulpwood to supply 21 million tons of paper and 23 million tons of paperboard. This estimate corresponds to more than double the 5 billion board feet of saw-

[19] NATIONAL HOUSING AGENCY. HOUSING FACTS. Washington. 1946.

and also with the volume of construction. There is likely to be some further displacement of wood piling by concrete and steel, and more of the wood piling will be given longer life by preservative treatment. Nevertheless, the estimate of potential requirements is substantially higher than present consumption.

Estimates of potential requirements for fence posts, mine timbers, and hardwood distillation are in line with present consumption. Some increase may be expected in demand for logs and bolts for specialized industries. On the other hand, potential requirements for hewn railroad ties and cooperage stock are estimated at less than present consumption.

Losses

Growth goals should, of course, include allowance for unpreventable losses from fire, insect and disease epidemics, and other natural causes. For the years 1934–43, annual losses due to fire and other destructive agents were 1.5 billion cubic feet of all timber, including 4.2 billion board feet of saw timber. Widespread application of good forestry should cut the rate of unsalvaged losses per million feet of growing stock in half. But because attainment of a larger growth goal involves a substantial increase in the volume subject to loss in the East, it does not seem advisable to bank on losses being less than 1.3 billion cubic feet, including 3.2 billion board feet of saw timber.

Ineffective Growth

The goals allow for growth that will not be available for use. One example is growth on land that may be set aside as roadside strips, parks, and other scenic areas, and so withdrawn from commercial use. Another example is growth coming up on formerly cultivated lands that may be cleared again before the timber is mature. A further allowance is made for growth occurring on timber too scattered for economic operation, in isolated or inferior stands that may remain permanently inaccessible, or in residual trees of inferior species or poor quality that are lost if they are not marketed along with the better trees with which they are mixed.

New Uses

Technological advances promise new uses for wood in addition to those envisaged in the foregoing estimates. During the war many ways were found to use wood in place of other materials that were in short supply. Permanent scarcity of nonrenewable materials may increase the opportunity for wood use.

For one thing, wood is being adapted to many new construction uses. Laminated wood arches, for instance, have proved satisfactory in such wide-roofed buildings as gymnasiums and auditoriums. The range of wood use is also being extended by new methods of gluing, by improved connecting devices and structural design, and by wider use of plywood.

Just beginning to be understood are the commercial possibilities of new processes that change the physical characteristics of wood. By chemical treatment, heat, and pressure, wood may be converted into new materials of great utility and promise. It may be rendered impervious to moisture, acid, and other chemicals. It may be molded into a variety of shapes. Specific gravity can be varied from section to section of the same piece—a property of special significance for such items as airplane propellers. It can be given a variety of attractive and desirable finishes—including color, figured veneer, stencil designs, etc.—all incorporated in the material so as to be as durable and washable as the material itself.

Beyond this, the outlook is bright for wood as a chemical raw material. Under the stimulus of war, initial plant installations have been made for manufacturing industrial ethyl alcohol from sawmill and pulp-mill waste. Ethyl alcohol, in addition to supplying many other commercial demands, may be used in the manufacture of rubber. Associated with the manufacture of alcohol from wood are the possibilities of developing a highly efficient source of food protein by growing yeast on wood sugar. The Germans carried this process past the experimental stage during the war. Generation of other products in the fermentation of wood cellulose may also lead to an increase in wood use. The possibilities are revolutionary in their implications, and tonnage requirements are unpredictable.

Lignin, the wood constituent next in importance to cellulose, is now largely wasted because its chemical structure is obscure. But chemists have begun to penetrate its mysteries. Lignin has been found valuable as binding material for road surfaces, in reducing the amount of lead needed in storage batteries, as a dispersing agent for cement in making concrete, and in plastics. Once understood, this plentiful byproduct, which now pollutes some of our rivers, may find wide beneficial use.

To the extent that new chemical processes make use of waste, they would not increase forest drain. However, some of the new products may become sufficiently important to call for additional timber cutting operations. It is not feasible to make a specific estimate of potential requirements for such uses, but they merit consideration in setting long-range growth goals.

National Security

The war showed what it means not to have enough timber to go around. The Nation learned how essential its forests are for military operations.

Every phase of the war—every operation—depended in some measure upon wood. Every freighter that left port with war supplies carried some 10 carloads of dunnage to pack and stabilize its cargo. Army cantonment construction required about 1,500 board feet of lumber per man. For every man sent overseas, 300 board feet was needed to box and crate his initial supplies, and it took nearly 50 board feet a month thereafter to keep him supplied. Every 2½-ton truck manufactured and shipped meant, on an average, the use of 1,000 feet of lumber. The smokeless powder in every 90,000 rounds of rifle ammunition, the paper in every lot of 4,200 weather-proof packages of blood plasma, took a cord of pulpwood. Furthermore, until lumber and other timber products themselves became difficult to obtain, the Nation looked to wood as a substitute for steel and other materials wherever possible.

The importance of adequate timber growth in national security is emphasized by prospective shortages of other strategic materials. Geologists predict exhaustion of domestic petroleum supplies in the foreseeable future. If abundant timber is at hand, alcohol made from wood could be used as fuel for internal-combustion engines. Furthermore, many of the byproducts of both coal and petroleum may be obtained also from wood. Dependence upon imports for such vital materials as rubber also affects national security. To the extent that such materials can be obtained from wood, the Nation could prepare to get along without imports by accumulating a backlog of accessible growing stock, which would not be drawn upon in time of peace.

To permit stock-piling of timber on the stump for emergency needs, annual timber growth should be higher than peacetime requirements.

Foreign Markets and Supplies

In setting long-range goals for the United States it is necessary to ask: will there be a world surplus of timber? If so, part of the United States' supply can continue to come from imports. Or will the rest of the world have less than it needs, so that there will be opportunity for larger export from this country?

The softwood forests of the North Temperate Zone, which comprise less than one-third of the world's forests, are by far the most important sources of the world's timber supply. Before the war almost 40 percent of the world's output of sawn timber was produced in the United States, and a little more than that in Europe. The rest of the world, mainly Canada and Japan, sawed only about 15 percent.

Furthermore, the war taught the importance of accessibility—having timber of the right size and right kind available at the right place for immediate use. Spruce was cut and brought from Alaska because accessible supplies in the Pacific Northwest were insufficient; large timbers and piling that should have been available for use in the South were cut and shipped there from the Pacific Northwest. Railroad facilities, urgently needed to haul food, equipment, and other war material, were too often tied up in transporting from distant regions lumber and other forest products that might have been grown closer to the point of consumption.

The bulk of the world's timber output is consumed in the countries where it grows. Only about 15 percent of the industrial timber (mostly sawn) has ever been exported in any one year. In 1935–38 the annual volume of international trade in sawn timber was about 12 or 13 billion board feet, 90 percent of which was softwood. Although historically an exporter of sawn timber, the United States imported more than it exported during both world wars. Considering wood in all forms, including pulp, the United States has imported more than it exported for the last 30 years or more.

Timber for general construction purposes is scarce throughout most of the civilized world. The more densely populated foreign countries have no prospect of fully supplying their own needs. World demand for softwoods will increase as industrialization spreads and living standards are raised. There is no indication that tropical hardwoods can take the place of the softwood forests of the North Temperate Zone. They will continue to be used primarily as special-purpose woods. In this situation the United States can count on export markets in the future for as much surplus general-purpose timber as she may be able to grow, provided this is made available at prices that foreign buyers can pay. Conversely, it will not be safe to count on imports to the extent that we have in recent years.

Canada has been the chief source of imports by the United States. In Canada, as in this country, the supply of operable timber has been diminishing in volume and deteriorating in quality for many years. Nevertheless, her own timber needs are expanding and she may increase her output. The bulk of Canada's lumber export goes to the United Kingdom, but part of her surplus will doubtless come to the United States. Furthermore, for perhaps 20 years it should be possible to get somewhat more pulp and paper, especially newsprint, from Canada.

Some consumers in the United States have turned to Central and South America for timber, but shipments from this direction are not likely to be large and will be chiefly hardwood. Industrial development in Central and South America is sure to increase domestic markets for timber. Only Brazil, which has extensive forests of araucaria (Paraná pine), and Mexico have much softwood timber to export. Brazil's export to her neighbors and to Europe and South Africa is likely to increase. But other countries to the south are likely to look to the United States for more softwood lumber than in the past. South America will, however, continue to export tropical woods for specialty uses.

Europe, which as a whole was self-sufficient in timber before the war, will need to import heavily for a long time. The needs for reconstruction are great and output on the whole is likely to be less than before the war. Sweden, Finland, and Russia are the only countries with resources to permit an increased cut. Sweden's output of logs and pulpwood was curtailed during the war by lack of shipping and the productive capacity of her forests was raised by increased cutting of fuel wood, chiefly in thinnings and improvement cuttings. The situation was similar in Finland, where prewar cut was less than sustained-yield capacity, but some of her forests suffered heavy war damage.

Although the forests of European Russia were generally being overcut before the war, and military operations destroyed much forest from the Baltic to the Black Sea, Russia is likely to increase her output. However, it is doubtful if she can produce enough to meet her own reconstruction needs. In the more distant future, growing domestic requirements are likely to keep pace with Russia's output and so hold down her export.

The countries most in need of imports are the United Kingdom, France and the Low Countries. The United Kingdom, which normally produces less than 5 percent of her timber consumption, had to fall back on her own forests during the war. More than two-thirds of the standing softwood timber and almost as large a proportion of the hardwoods were cut. Many of the forests of France, Belgium, and the Netherlands were heavily damaged. In all these countries the need for reconstruction is great. Germany and the Mediterranean countries are also in need of timber. However, Germany's growing stock was not greatly impaired by the war, and her forests should be able to take care of most of her reconstruction needs.

In Asia, the forests of the U. S. S. R. are largely undeveloped. A growing population and industrial development are creating a large domestic demand for wood. Any surplus in the Urals and Western Siberia probably would go to European Russia. The extensive forests of Eastern Siberia can produce much more than is likely to be required locally. This will help take care of the needs of China, Korea, and Japan, which should be the natural markets for it. On the other hand, the vast interior forests of Siberia, thousands of miles from good seaports and mostly lacking railroads, seem unlikely to provide much timber for export.

China will need large quantities of timber. Some of this may be supplied from Siberia, the Netherlands East Indies, and the Philippines. But China will doubtless continue to seek imports from western Canada and the United States.

Before the war Japan's forests furnished 90 percent of the timber she used, but cutting has been heavy since 1932. Her requirements to rebuild demolished cities and shipping will be great. Unless her standard of living is to remain permanently much below the prewar level, Japan will need fairly large timber imports.

India and the other countries of southeastern Asia, except Burma and Siam, may need to import timber if they develop industrially. The East Indies and the Philippines have large undeveloped forests which contain much valuable timber. These countries should be able to help supply the growing demands of China and southeastern Asia. Their exports to Europe and the United States are likely to be chiefly high-grade specialty woods.

Australia and New Zealand have never exported much lumber, except to each other, and are not likely to do so. Both import much softwood from western United States and Canada. Extensive planting of conifers may eventually enable them to become self-sufficient.

The countries of northern, eastern, and southern Africa can never furnish large quantities of timber. Their own needs are likely to increase and they will probably always need to import. Western and central Africa, however, have large tropical forests and may eventually export from half a billion to a billion board feet of hardwood to Europe and America.

With the world's timber situation as it is, the United States has much to gain from building up its resources to the point where it will have a substantial margin for export. This may even be viewed as a moral obligation, for by making its full contribution to the world's timber needs the United States will be working for peace in an important way.

Goal Is To Double Saw-Timber Growth

It has been feasible to make quantitative estimates only for potential requirements and for losses from fire, insects, diseases, and other natural causes. Between the sum of these estimates and the upper range of the proposed goal (p. 33), the margin for ineffective growth, new uses, national security, and export is about 4 billion cubic feet, or 8 billion board feet:

Item:	All timber (billion cu. ft.)	Saw timber (billion bd. ft.)
Timber products	14.6	61.0
Losses	1.3	3.2
Margin	4.1	7.8
Total	20.0	72.0

The Forest Service regards this as a reasonable allowance, and hence has made its calculations on the basis of the upper range.

A quantitative growth goal is suggested with full realization of the uncertainties involved, but with the conviction that this is needed to give point and perspective to the forest situation. Some students of the situation may prefer to set up as the objective the bringing of all commercial forest lands to full productivity. This would mean setting higher figures and would require a longer time for achievement. Others may prefer a lower goal—for example, the lower range of 18 billion cubic feet and 65 billion board feet mentioned on p. 33. This of course involves reducing either the figure for potential requirements or the margin for unestimated factors. This lower goal could be reached sooner, but when everything is taken into consideration, the character and magnitude of needed action for the next several decades would be about the same.

To achieve the goal suggested means increasing all-timber growth 50 percent and doubling saw-timber growth.

The importance of having plenty of saw timber in the growth goal can hardly be overemphasized. A large part of our timber need is, and probably always will be, for the kind of material that comes from big trees. Moreover, one way to keep logging costs down is to manage forests so that the bulk of the crop can be cut from trees of saw-timber size. Even for products like pulpwood, for which trees of saw-timber size are not essential, large trees are generally less expensive to handle.

The significance of the growth goals in relation to current growth can be clarified by considering the situation by regions. The allocation of growth goals to regions suggested in table 15 is in no sense a forecast. It is intended only as a reasonable illustration of how the various regions might participate in the national goals, taking into account the acreage of commercial forest land, the potential rate of growth in the principal types, local accessibility, ease of management, and position with respect to consuming markets.

About half of the goal is assigned to the South, which has some 40 percent of the commercial forest land, very favorable growing conditions, and easy access to important consuming regions.

The increase in growth of *all timber* suggested for the South is almost 60 percent; for the North

it is about 25 percent. The suggested increase is only about 20 percent in the Rocky Mountain regions but about 100 percent for California and the Pacific Northwest.

To meet the suggested allocation of *saw-timber* goals, growth will need to be almost doubled in the South, more than doubled in the North, and increased to 2½ times its present volume in the West.

These goals present a real challenge to forestry in this country. Certainly we need not fear timber surplus. The goals would not be vitiated if demand should fall below annual growth in periods of economic depression. The resulting increase in growing stock would simply put the country in position to achieve the goals sooner.

Finally, goals that call for keeping the land well-stocked and for maintaining a large volume of saw timber will best promote other forest values. In general, the better the cover the better the watershed protection; and the bigger the timber the more attractive the forest to the people.

TABLE 15.—*Growth goals and current annual timber growth by regions*

Section and region	All timber		Saw timber	
	Growth goal	Current growth	Growth goal	Current growth
	Billion cu. ft.	*Billion cu. ft.*	*Billion bd. ft.*	*Billion bd. ft.*
North:				
New England	1.14	0.90	4.0	1.8
Middle Atlantic	1.64	1.40	5.8	2.7
Lake	1.15	.81	3.1	1.4
Central	1.73	1.44	4.5	2.3
Plains	.12	.12	.2	.2
Total	5.78	4.67	17.6	8.4
South:				
South Atlantic	2.14	1.76	7.8	6.1
Southeast	4.80	2.71	17.5	8.2
West Gulf	3.20	1.92	12.1	5.6
Total	10.14	6.39	37.4	19.9
West:				
Pacific Northwest:				
Douglas-fir subregion	2.17	1.02	10.0	3.7
Pine subregion	.38	.22	1.4	.5
Total	2.55	1.24	11.4	4.2
California	.64	.33	2.8	1.2
North Rocky Mtn.	.65	.54	1.9	1.3
South Rocky Mtn.	.24	.20	.9	.3
Total	4.08	2.31	17.0	7.0
United States	20.00	13.37	72.0	35.3

The Problem of Meeting Timber Needs

Goals are suggested in the preceding section as a basis for sound national policy. To achieve these goals saw-timber growth will have to be doubled. As things are going now there is no prospect that this will be accomplished in the foreseeable future. But if positive measures to maintain and build forest productivity were promptly and generally applied throughout the Nation, this goal could be attained, although it would take time. The size of the task can be clarified by inquiring how much growing stock will be required and by outlining broadly a feasible course of physical progress toward the objective.

What Growing Stock Is Needed To Double Saw-Timber Growth?

As previously pointed out, sustained yield requires a reasonable balance of age classes, from seedlings up to the age at which the more exacting products can best be obtained. Since growing stock is the sum of the volumes in all age classes, the growing stock needed to sustain a given annual yield will depend largely upon the cutting age for the final crop harvested. For saw timber of desirable size in the various forest types and regions this ranges from 60 to 140 years. To a lesser extent growing stock will depend upon the proportion of the total harvest that can be obtained from thinnings or improvement cuttings. Fast-growing species require less growing stock than slow-growing species because they attain a size suitable for a given product at an earlier age. Conversely, adverse climate and soil increase the amount of growing stock required because they limit the growth rate.

In the South, where growth is generally rapid and an appreciable part of the harvest may be taken from thinnings or other intermediate cutting, only 16 to 18 board feet should be needed as growing stock for each board foot of annual drain. At the other extreme, in the South Rocky Mountain region, because of slow growth and less favorable markets for small trees, the saw-timber growing stock will need to be 50 times the annual drain.

The growing stock needed to yield 72 billion board feet of annual growth allocated as suggested in the previous section appears to be 1,700 billion board feet (table 16). About 40 percent of this is allotted to the West and 60 percent to the East.

TABLE 16.—*Minimum growing stock to sustain future growth goals*

Section and region	Volume	Multiple of present stand
	Billion bd. ft.	*Number*
North:		
New England	87	1.50
Middle Atlantic	128	2.06
Lake	86	1.72
Central	99	2.25
Plains	6	1.00
Total	406	1.85
South:		
South Atlantic	127	1.31
Southeast	284	2.09
West Gulf	210	2.00
Total	621	1.84
West:		
Pacific Northwest:		
Douglas-fir subregion	350	0.69
Pine subregion	70	.56
Total	420	.67
California	129	.57
North Rocky Mtn.	79	.62
South Rocky Mtn.	45	.79
Total	673	.65
United States	1,700	1.06

The North and South now have little more than half enough saw timber to sustain their suggested share of the growth goal (fig. 11). A 469-billion-board-foot deficit in these sections is partially offset by the fact that the West has 370 billion

40

board feet more than is needed for its share of the goal. However, as previously noted, much of the western timber is inactive capital in the virgin stands. If only the second-growth saw timber there is considered, the active growing stock is 235 billion board feet or only 35 percent of what it would be necessary to develop by judicious selective cutting in the virgin stands and by establishing new stands on clear-cut areas.

These estimates of the growing stock needed to realize the growth objectives assume a proper distribution of timber sizes. They assume also that the virgin timber will have been converted to active growing stock. To the extent that these assumptions are not fulfilled, the volume of growing stock would need to be higher. On the other hand, if more intensive forest management should increase the proportion of yield from thinnings and improvement cuttings, or if new utilization practices should reduce the cutting ages for final harvest, less growing stock would be required.

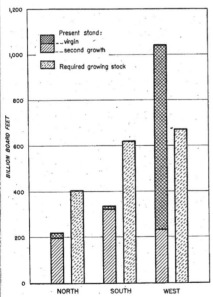

FIGURE 11.—*Present saw-timber stand, and growing stock needed to sustain the growth goals.*

806034°—49——4

In any event, it is clear that the growing stock should be increased. However large the present stand looms in relation to current consumption, it is not enough to yield an annual crop of the size suggested in the goals. Indeed, with growing stock in the North and South so deficient it is doubly fortunate that there is some residue of virgin timber to supplement growth through the next few decades.

When Could the Growth Goal Be Reached?

A comprehensive program dealing adequately with all phases of a sustained timber supply would imply, for example, that all the forests would be well protected, that destructive cutting would be stopped, that at least 400 million acres would be managed so as to build up growing stock and output; that from 20 to 25 percent of the land would be under very intensive management, that planting of nonproductive lands would be undertaken on an unprecedented scale, and that access road construction in the West would be continued on a large scale. Assuming all these things, how much timber could be budgeted for harvesting each year, and how rapidly could the objectives in saw-timber growth be reached?

No hard and fast answer can be given. But enough is known about the condition of the forests and their potential growth capacity to give the theoretical limits of accomplishment if the Nation were to embark on a course such as that suggested above. Calculations of saw-timber growing stock in each region have been carried forward for 75 years, balancing the growth that might be realized under such a comprehensive forestry program against an assumed saw-timber drain, decade by decade. A major consideration was to keep the annual output as high as possible without precluding the possibility of reaching the regional growth goal in 75 years. The story is told graphically in figure 12.

For the first 30 years, drain might remain higher than annual growth chiefly because of the large contribution virgin timber could make to the total cut in the early decades. From the outset, however, growth would be increasing and before the end of the century it might be some 10 billion board feet above the assumed annual drain.

Under a comprehensive forest program, timber

growth might advance to about 64 billion board feet in 45 years. This is the level of estimated potential requirements plus losses, with no margin for security, export, new uses, or ineffective growth. If that amount should prove sufficient for all our needs, annual drain could then be increased to 64 billion board feet and annual growth would level off, as indicated by the light lines in figure 12. However, to attain a 72-billion-board-foot goal annual drain would have to remain below annual growth for 25 to 30 years longer, in order to build up more growing stock.

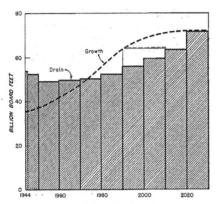

FIGURE 12.—*Theoretical course of annual saw-timber growth and drain in the United States under a comprehensive forestry program designed to achieve 72-billion-board-foot growth goal in 75 years with minimum reduction of output in the years immediately ahead.*

It is important to emphasize that the course of annual growth depicted here assumes widespread and prompt application of good forest practices. It is very improbable that this assumption will become a reality; hence the indicated course of annual growth is above what is likely to occur. These calculations, like the growth goals themselves, serve to give perspective but represent only one possible outcome. They visualize achieving the growth goals in 75 years with minimum disruption of forest industries and markets. Cutting more heavily than indicated, for any extended period, might delay or preclude the increase in annual growth envisioned for the North and South. It might lead to a protracted period of greatly reduced cut in the West, should

the virgin timber be exhausted before new growth was ready to support the indicated sustained volume of output. On the other hand, several years of greatly reduced output in a depression like that of the thirties might result in building up growing stocks, and hence annual growth, faster than shown in figure 12. Protracted reduction of output resulting from disproportionately high prices for timber products would have a similar effect.

Where Shall We Get Timber Products in the Meantime?

The preceding discussion reveals the dilemma that the Nation's forest situation presents: The calculations of what can be safely cut if forest productivity is to be built up indicate that annual drain should be less than 50 billion board feet for perhaps 30 years (fig. 12). This is 4 billion feet below the 1944 drain. Yet there is an urgent need for greater output. To what extent will efforts to satisfy present needs further impair future productivity? If the Nation exercises sufficient restraint to avoid continued overcutting, would that mean permanent loss of markets for wood by forcing people to use other materials?

The possible output of the different sections of the country under the comprehensive forestry program visualized in the preceding discussion throws some light on these questions (fig. 13).

Eastern output cannot be maintained.—Sixty-three percent of the saw-timber drain, and a still larger part of all-timber drain, takes place in the North and South. Under the impact of this drain the already inadequate growing stock is diminishing; yet in the allocation of the saw-timber growth goal it was suggested that the forests of the North should support twice the 1944 drain and those in the South 50 percent more. To accomplish this will require that growing stock be built up, and that in turn can be done only by cutting less than is cut now. Indeed, it seems likely, because of growing-stock shortages, that output from the North and South will be forced down in the decade ahead. With good forest practices this decline need not go more than 5 billion board feet below the 1944 level, but there is little prospect that output could safely be boosted again for 20 or 30 years. Still, with economic activity continuing at a high level the depleted growing stock is going to be under constant pressure for overcutting, and it is very doubtful that as favorable a course as that suggested can be achieved.

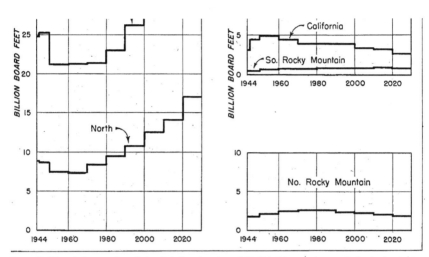

FIGURE 13.—*Theoretical course of saw-timber drain in various parts of the United States under a comprehensive forestry program designed to achieve 72-billion-board-foot growth in 75 years with minimum reduction of output in the years immediately ahead.*

Western development could help bridge the gap.—Obviously the West, which has 65 percent of the present saw-timber stand but accounts for only 37 percent of the drain, must supply a larger part of our national needs during the next few decades. But it should be recognized that the special values inherent in the high-quality virgin timber will never be replaced. The need to maintain output should be balanced against the desirability of making this high-quality virgin timber last just as long as possible. Dependent western communities should also be protected from excessive timber depletion that would rob them of the means of existence.

Fortunately a large part of the timber still awaiting access to market is on the national forests

and other public land. With private timber playing out, the public forests are becoming more important in the current timber supply. For example, saw timber in public ownership in the Pacific Northwest rose from 54 percent of the total during the middle thirties to 63 percent in 1945. The increasing importance of public timber in the West places a new responsibility on public forest managers.

Between World Wars I and II the lumber industry was often in difficulty because its plant capacity exceeded the market for its products. With private timber under pressure to be cut and the industry in a generally shaky position, the sale of national-forest timber and the opening up of new units proceeded slowly. Furthermore, among private owners there was widespread opposition to the sale of public timber. But as timber shortage came to be widely felt, the Forest Service adopted a policy of obtaining from each forest the maximum possible output consistent with sustained-yield management. This involves a great expansion in timber survey and management plan work. It means taking every opportunity to cull decadent timber from otherwise vigorous stands and to make desirable thinnings in young stands. It calls for a far-flung road-building program to gain access to undeveloped areas.

Financing of access-road construction, given impetus during the war and assumed in part by the National Housing Agency in 1947, has subsequently fallen far below what is needed. Extending roads rapidly into undeveloped localities helps spin out the old growth by making it possible to spread the cut over a wider area. It permits salvaging of bug-killed timber before it rots. It enables marketing of a large volume of inferior species hitherto untouched. It facilitates selective cutting in types adapted to it, thus adding to the effective annual growth.

Although the volume of virgin timber in the West is substantial, the opportunities for greater output are limited. The national-forest cut is already more than double what it was before the war and may eventually be doubled again. The cut from other public lands may also be increased. But this is sure to be offset, in part, by a decline in the cut from private lands. The situation in most of the older lumber-producing localities is precarious. Lack of stumpage has caused many mills to shut down in recent years and this process is likely to be accelerated.

In the Pacific Northwest, depletion has already progressed so far that there is little hope of substantial increase in saw-timber cut (fig. 13). New opportunities for large-scale operation, generally dependent upon construction of access roads, are confined largely to southwestern Oregon, where sawmill capacity has already reached the sustained-yield capacity of the forest. It is doubtful whether increased output from southwestern Oregon can offset the inevitable decline in the older localities farther north. Indeed, considering the region as a whole, operation for a few decades at the present rate would so reduce the timber supply that output would need to taper off, perhaps, to some 3 billion feet below the 1944 level. This would

bring it down to the level suggested in the allocation of the growth goals.

In the North Rocky Mountains, more access roads and utilization of the less-favored species may increase the cut almost 1 billion board feet annually for 30 to 40 years. But after that, output might taper off again to somewhere near the 1944 levels. Similarly, if economic conditions permit, the output of the South Rocky Mountain region could be doubled. But that would represent a gain of only 0.5 billion board feet. Increasing the cut in these regions is not simple. Much of of the timber is of little-used species and in light stands. A good part of it is on rough, rocky ground where logging will involve more expense than is usual at present.

California—in spite of prospective shortages in several of its producing centers, and operating conditions often as difficult as in the Rocky Mountain regions—seems to have the timber to permit, with good forestry, increased output in the years ahead. If access roads were built to open up the remaining virgin areas in the course of 30 to 40 years, and if partial cutting were generally applied, the effective annual growth would soon assume large proportions. Drain, reported at 3.1 billion board feet in 1944, could increase to 5 billion board feet 20 years hence. However, after the virgin stands had all been worked over, output would need to drop again, probably to somewhat below the 1944 figure.

Summing up the situation nationally, the calculations indicate that for the next 30 years the largest feasible output from the West under a constructive program of forestry will not fully offset the necessary reduction of output in the East. The indicated drain of about 50 billion board feet would ordinarily include a lumber output of 30 to 31 billion board feet, which is less than current consumption, to say nothing of the goal.

Alaska can contribute pulpwood.—Alaskan timber resources have not yet been tapped on a large scale. The accessible timber occurs in a narrow fringe of the national forests along the tidewater of southeastern Alaska. It is chiefly valuable as pulpwood. The bulk of it is western hemlock, intermixed on the better sites with Sitka spruce—often of large size and high quality—and some cedar.

Forest Service policy calls for the establishment of pulp mills in Alaska as the foundation for in-

about 7 percent of the potential pulp-
rements.

rospects are limited.—As indicated in
section, there is less opportunity to
iports than might be supposed. All
e is a world shortage as well as a do-
tage of timber. So it will be wise to
:ogram that would eventually enable
7. to be self-sufficient and also to con-
he needs of other nations.

The Job Is a Big One

the preceding calculations are hypo-
y make it clear that if the goals are to be
ie Nation has a tremendous job to do.
e decades of good forestry, going far

now denuded or only poorly stocked with
lings and saplings would lay the foundation fo:
ditional timber growth in the future. But
proved forest practices applied to the ti:
now standing are the surest and quickest m
of increasing annual growth. To provide
security of an adequate timber supply, the N:
must have a more dynamic national policy w
will prevent unsatisfactory forest practices
obtain a much wider application of susta
yield management. Some of the land now in
vate ownership will need to be shifted to p:
ownership. All of these things take time tc
under way; and once under way, they re:
more time to achieve their purpose. The:
no easy way out.

How Timberlands Are Being Managed

➤➤➤ ━━━━━━━━━━━━━━━━━━━━━━━━━━━━━━━━━━━━ ◄◄◄

The United States has been slow in facing up to the hard fact that to produce timber in ample, sustained quantities requires purposeful management—real forestry.

The job to be done is not so much one of establishing new forests (although this, too, has its place) as it is of properly treating and utilizing those we have. A great deal depends on timber-cutting practices; on whether the amount of cut is adjusted to the rate of growth; on the quality of protection; on the aims and policies of the forest owner.

Many people take it for granted that a reasonably satisfactory brand of forestry is practiced on much of our timber-producing land. A Nationwide survey, made by the Forest Service in cooperation with other Federal, State, and private agencies as part of the Reappraisal,[20] shows that actually there is good forestry on only a small part of it. Limited to commercial forest lands, this survey considered publicly owned land and private holdings of 50,000 acres or more on a 100-percent basis. The remaining private land was covered by sampling methods; in all, some 42,000 small and medium-sized holdings, distributed to give fair representation by size of property and region, were examined. The survey dealt with: (1) The character of recent timber-cutting practices, (2) the extent to which the larger holdings are being managed for sustained yield, and (3) the quality of fire protection.

Timber-Cutting Practices Are Far From Satisfactory

The following criteria were used in rating cutting practice:

1. *High-order cutting* requires the best types

[20] Results of this survey are more fully covered in Reappraisal Report 3. The Management Status of Forest Lands in the United States. U. S. Forest Service. 1946.

of harvest cutting which will maintain quality and quantity yields consistent with the full productive capacity of the land. Wherever needed, it requires cultural practices such as planting, timber-stand-improvement cuttings, thinnings, and control of grazing.

2. *Good cutting* requires good silviculture that leaves the land in possession of desirable species in condition for vigorous growth in the immediate future. It is substantially better than fair cutting.

3. *Fair cutting* marks the beginning of cutting practices which will maintain on the land any reasonable stock of growing timber in species that are desirable and marketable.

4. *Poor cutting* leaves the land with a limited means for natural reproduction, often in the form of remnant seed trees. It often causes deterioration of species with consequent reduction in both quality and quantity of forest growth.

TABLE 17.—*Character of timber cutting on commercial forest land by ownership class, 1945*

Ownership class	Commercial forest area		Character of cutting [1]				
	Total	Operating	High-order	Good	Fair	Poor	Destructive
	Million acres	Million acres	Percent	Percent	Percent	Percent	Percent
All lands	461	403	3	20	25	46	6
Private	345	302	1	7	28	56	8
Public	116	101	8	59	19	13	1
National forest	74	65	11	69	19	1	0
Other Federal	15	12	6	37	32	24	1
State and local	27	24	3	44	10	41	2

[1] Percents shown refer to the operating acreage in each class now being managed under cutting practices that rate high-order, good, etc.

5. *Destructive cutting* leaves the land without timber values and without means for natural reproduction.

Ratings were applied to the entire acreage of "operating" forest properties, taking national forests and other very large properties by working circles. In the aggregate this included about nine-tenths of all commercial forest land in the North and South and eight-tenths in the West. "Non-operating" included tracts not operated for timber, those where fire or other agents had obscured evidences of cutting, and some remote national-forest lands that await access roads to open them for logging.

More than half of all recent cutting was rated "poor" or "destructive" (table 17). Less than one-fourth of the cutting measures up to good forestry standards.

Character of cutting practices varies greatly by ownership class. On the public lands cutting is notably better than that on private lands. Two-thirds of the cutting is rated good or better, only 14 percent poor or destructive. But only about one-fourth of the commercial acreage and a much smaller fraction of potential timber growing capacity is publicly owned.

Moreover, on some public land there is much room for improvement. Good to high-order practices have yet to be attained in 25 percent of the cutting on western national forests, and on much of the 15 million acres of other Federal lands, where one-fourth of the cutting is poor and destructive. For the 27 million acres of State and local government lands, 43 percent of the cutting is in the latter categories (fig. 14).

The practices on the 345 million acres of private timberlands carry most weight since these forests will remain our principal source of timber. Gen-

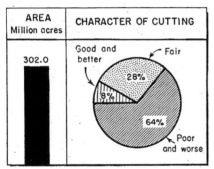

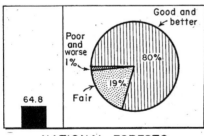

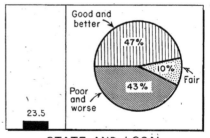

FIGURE 14.—*Operating area and character of cutting by ownership class, 1945.*

erally speaking, they are the accessible, potentially more productive lands and until recently some 90 percent or more of our timber cut has come from them.

It is largely the poor practices on most private lands that make the national showing unfavorable. About two-thirds of the cutting in private forests rates poor and destructive, hence will not keep the land reasonably productive. Although the other one-third will probably maintain a reasonably acceptable growing stock, only 8 percent is good or better.

Large private owners, on the average, treat their lands better than the small owners (table 18). Only 32 percent of the cutting on the large properties is poor or destructive while 29 percent rates good or better. These properties, however, include only about one-seventh of the private lands;

they are held by about 400 of the 4,226,000 forest owners.

TABLE 18.--Character of timber cutting on private lands by size of holding,[1] 1945

Size of holding	Commercial forest area		Character of cutting				
	Total	Oper-ating	High-order	Good	Fair	Poor	De-struc-tive
	Million acres	Million acres	Percent	Percent	Percent	Percent	Percent
Small	261	224	0	4	25	63	8
Medium	33	29	1	7	31	50	11
Large	51	49	5	24	39	28	4

[1] Small=less than 5,000 acres (4,222,000 owners); medium=5,000 and up to 50,000 acres (3,200 owners); large=50,000 acres and more (400 owners).

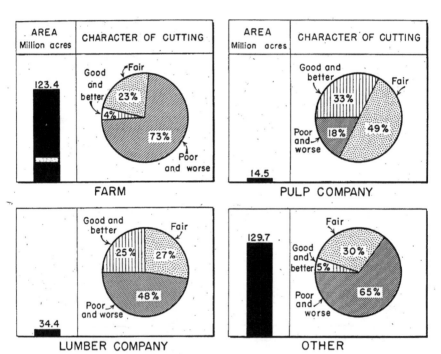

FIGURE 15.—Private operating area and character of cutting by type of owner, 1945.

Miscellaneous Publication 668, U. S. Department of Agriculture

properties or working circles that still have a back-log of virgin timber, the cutting should be so planned that when the virgin timber is gone, annual harvests commensurate with the inherent productivity of the land may be obtained from second growth, without drastic readjustment of output.

Sustained-yield ratings were applied only to public forest lands and to about 25 percent of the private holdings—those of 5,000 acres or more. These lands have the greater part of the good and high-order cutting. The small holdings were not rated because the evidences of sustained-yield were not recognizable, in most cases. Some doubtless are being managed on a sustained-yield basis. Lands were classified in the sustained yield category when there was recognizable evidence of a planned, continuous flow of products in substantially regular or increasing quantities—provided the cutting practice was at least fair.

The data show that about two-fifths of the operating acreage in public ownership and nearly three-fourths of that in the medium and large private holdings is not on a sustained-yield basis.

Ownership class:	Percent of cutting on sustained-yield, basis, 1945 [1]
Public	57
National forest	72
Other Federal	44
State and local	23
Private (holdings of 5,000 acres and more)	28
Medium	9
Large	39

[1] Weighted in accordance with the number of acres in each operating property or working circle.

National forests make the best showing with 72 percent. About one-fourth of the cutting on State and local government lands is rated on a sustained-yield basis.

Most national-forest land not on sustained yield is in remote localities in the West. Actually, these lands are under management which assures future output of forest products and services. They are well protected. Cutting policies are well established. But the lack of access roads and other economic factors have held cutting below sustained-yield capacity. These limitations likewise apply to some extent on other public and some private lands.

Sustained-yield management has made considerable progress on the large private holdings, with 39 percent in this category. But the owners of medium-sized holdings as a group have hardly begun sustained-yield cutting; it is practiced on only 9 percent of their holdings.

The proportion of sustained-yield practice varies considerably in different parts of the country. In the South all the cutting on national-forest lands is on a sustained-yield basis; in the North, 75 percent; and in the West, 65. For the large private holdings the corresponding break-down is: South 61 percent, North 32, and West 3.

Although significant progress has been made in the Douglas-fir subregion, these figures indicate that for the West as a whole private owners have attained little sustained-yield management. The progress in management made by industry in the West as a whole. appears to have been largely in the field of fire protection and to a lesser extent in planning for new crops on cut-over lands rather than in adjusting current cutting to sustained-yield capacity.

The Status of Timber Management

To measure quality of timber management, three factors should be taken into consideration: (1) Cutting practice, (2) sustained yield, and (3) fire protection. Since it is was impracticable to apply the sustained-yield test to the 76 percent of private land in small holdings, a combination of cutting practice and fire protection ratings must suffice as the yardstick for this appraisal. In the field survey, protection was classified in four categories —good, fair, poor, and none—good protection being comparable to that on the better-protected public and private lands.

Combining the protection ratings with character of timber cutting, management grades were defined as follows:

1. *Intensive management* requires high-order cutting and good fire protection.
2. *Extensive management* requires at least fair cutting and fair fire protection.
   a. *Good extensive* requires good cutting as a minimum.
   b. *Fair extensive* requires fair cutting as a minimum.
3. *Without management* means that either the cutting practices or the fire protection, or both, rate poor or worse.
4. *Nonoperating area* means that the area is not being operated for timber products.

Only a little over one-third of the land is under timber management as thus defined (fig. 16). This includes only 2 percent intensively managed, 16

percent under good extensive management, and 17 percent under fair extensive management. More than half is without management; 13 percent is non-operating.

Only 14 percent of the publicly owned commercial forest land is without timber management, in contrast to 65 percent of the private land (table 19). Of the public lands, those in State and local government ownership rank below Federal forests in extent of management.

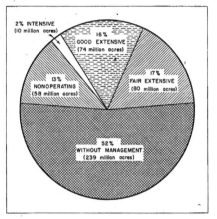

FIGURE 16.—*Management status of commercial forest lands, 1945.*

TABLE 19.—*Management status of commercial forest lands, 1945*

Ownership class	Commercial forest area	Management Grade				
		Intensive	Extensive		Without	Non-operating
			Good	Fair		
	Million acres	*Percent*	*Percent*	*Percent*	*Percent*	*Percent*
Private	345	1	4	18	65	12
Public	116	7	51	15	14	13[1]
National forest	74	9	61	17	1	12
Other Federal	15	3	31	19	28	19
State and local	27	2	37	8	40	13

[1] Part of these lands receives fire protection.

The management status of national forests is best in the North, where all of their acreage is under management—26 percent intensive and 74 percent extensive. In the South, about 32 percent is intensively managed and about 60 percent extensively managed.[21]

In the West, where almost three-fourths of the commercial acreage of the national forests is located, intensive timber management has hardly begun. Eighty-one percent is under extensive management. The rest is mostly in working circles where cutting has not been feasible. Most of the extensive management on national forests is characterized by good cutting practices.

Of the private lands, those held by large industrial owners show better management than do those held by small nonindustrial and farm owners. Seventy percent of the pulp-company lands are under management; but this can be said of little more than one-third of the lumber-company lands and only one-fifth of the other nonfarm and farm woodlands. The low rating for small owners is mainly because of poor cutting practices.

In the South only 19 percent of the private operating acreage is under management, as compared with 32 percent in the North and 38 percent in the West (table 20). In all three sections more than three-fifths of the operating area would be disqualified for management because of poor cutting practices. But in the South poor fire protection alone disqualifies an additional 17 percent.

The foregoing helps to show where we stand now in timber management. Since comparable information has not heretofore been obtained, we can draw few conclusions as to progress beyond certain generalizations:

As late as 1938 the Forest Service estimated that only about three-fifths of the commercial forest land in the national forests was in an active timber-operating status. But subsequently the strong demand for timber has enabled the Service to extend active timber management to about 88 percent of the commercial lands and to intensify management through timber-stand-improvement cuttings. Most of the nonoperating 12 percent is in the high mountains of the West.

There are also clear indications of progress on the large holdings of lumber and pulp companies. The forest industries have the assuring of raw-material supply as an incentive and are in a key position for practicing and demonstrating good forestry. They employed about 500 technical for-

[21] National forests contain but 5.6 percent of the commercial forest in the North, and 5.5 percent in the South.

esters in 1945 and now have many more. They are making headway but have a long way to go. And they own only 15 percent of the private timberland.

TABLE 20.—*Percent of private operating area with and without management, 1945*

Section	Intensive and extensive management	Without management		
		Poor cutting	Poor cutting and poor protection	Poor protection
	Percent	*Percent*	*Percent*	*Percent*
North	32	48	16	4
South	19	21	43	17
West	38	54	7	1

Much less encouraging is the situation with respect to small holdings, both farm and nonfarm. Only about 18 percent of these are under extensive management and a negligible percent is under intensive management. Even the publicly supported fire-control programs, on which steady progress has been made, are notably deficient in the South and in the Central region, where more than 60 percent of the acreage in small holdings is found.

Better management of forest lands is being furthered by various industry programs such as that of the American Forest Products Industries, the "Tree Farm" and "Keep Green" campaigns, and the efforts of the Southern Pulpwood Conservation Association. Publicly financed technical assistance in harvesting and marketing has been stepped up in recent years. All these are good so far as they go. But the job of reaching more than 4 million forest owners—of bringing the whole 345 million acres under good management—is big and difficult. Herein is one of the major challenges in American forestry.

Forest practices that keep the land at least reasonably productive are essential. Though limited as yet, there is enough good private forestry in all regions and among all classes of owners to show that it is practicable—that it pays and is good business. Yet many private owners are badly handicapped in practicing good forestry. And much remains to be done in fostering a better understanding of the opportunities in private forestry and of the need for good stewardship. It will take greatly increased public aid and encouragement to overcome these difficulties.

Forest Industries Based On Timber

The timber-products industries constitute one of the main channels through which the forests contribute to the economic life of the Nation. It is important, therefore, to examine the problem of timber supply in relation to these industries.

On the one hand we should have answers to such questions as these: Are the industries prepared to supply the Nation's potential requirements for timber products? What kind of timber do the industries need? What are their raw-material supply problems?

On the other hand we need to know how the pattern of industry development affects the timber resource and whether the industries are set up to provide economic outlets for what is being grown.

The Lumber Industry

Lumber manufacture is by far the largest of the wood-using industries. Its 39,000 establishments, employing an estimated 442,000 full-time equivalent workers and paying wages estimated at $774,000,000, accounted for 70 percent of the saw-timber cut in 1944.

There is an urgent demand for new housing. If we maintain a high-level economy there will be a large volume of other construction. The need for reconstruction abroad must also be considered. All together, real needs are likely to exceed the output of the lumber industry for many years.

Although per capita consumption has declined over a 40-year period, lumber is still the most widely used building material. It is the unrivaled material for many shipping purposes and finds its way into thousands of fabricated products.

Traditionally, the lumber industry has been migratory. The first sawmills in a pioneer region generally were small and served local needs. Later, the virgin timber was opened up on a large scale in order to supply other sections of the country. Large blocks of timber were accumulated or acquired by grant and these became the basis for large-mill operations. Heavy investments were made in transportation and logging facilities. The large mills tended to be clustered in strategic locations such as harbors, rivers, and rail centers. Financial pressure incident to the large investments generally tended to maintain output at a high level as long as timber was available in quantity. As the virgin timber disappeared the large mills were forced to close down. Usually, however, small blocks of timber were left because of ownership or other reasons, especially around the periphery of operations. Second growth, which was commonly neglected by the large mills, assumed increasing importance. Such timber continued to support small mills. In fact, being better adapted to cutting small blocks, scattered stands, and smaller timber, the little mills then came into their own.

Tractor logging and truck transportation have increased the flexibility of woods operations. They have made possible the economic logging of small parcels and of selected species or classes of timber that could not be handled with railroad logging. Such equipment has fostered small operations, enabling them to compete on more nearly equal terms.

The greater flexibility and mobility of logging operations increase the opportunity for good forest management and for using timber now wasted. But if not directed toward these ends, greater flexibility and mobility may, and do, lead to more destructive cutting and more complete depletion of forest growing stock.

Portable mills, most of which cut less than 1 million board feet a year, present difficult problems. Because they require little capital and are not exacting in log requirements, they open the lumber business to persons with little money and business experience. Equipment is often obsolete, poorly set up, or in need of repair. Manufacturing practice is commonly poor. Sawing for a restricted market, such as that for ties or dimension lumber, sometimes leads to excessive waste. Cost account-

are as a rule wasteful of timber, taking only the best in hard times and, when profits are high, cutting too fast and taking small timber which should be held as growing stock.

TABLE 21.—*Number of mills and percent of lumber cut, by size of mill,[1] 1942*

MILLS

Mill size	North	South	West	United States
	Number	*Number*	*Number*	*Number*
Small	17,031	18,529	2,331	37,891
Medium	78	419	294	791
Large	5	25	183	213
Total	17,114	18,973	2,808	38,895

LUMBER CUT

	Percent	*Percent*	*Percent*	*Percent*
Small	11.6	28.9	4.8	45.3
Medium	2.0	12.1	8.3	22.4
Large	.4	2.0	29.9	32.3
Total	14.0	43.0	43.0	100.0

[1] Small: Cutting less than 5 million board feet per year. Medium: Cutting between 5 and 25 million board feet per year. Large: Cutting more than 25 million board feet per year.

Within the limits of timber supply and available labor and equipment, excess mill capacity allows quick expansion of output in time of need or when markets are good. However, lumber output was only 76 percent of the 48 billion board feet of estimated practical capacity in 1942, the peak year of war production. It dropped to 59 percent of capacity in 1945 when labor and equipment were short. But in 1947, with lumber prices far above those of other building materials, output surpassed that of 1942. Nevertheless, it is increasingly clear that shortage of suitable available timber has held output back in many localities.

The excess capacity would appear much greater if estimates were based on a full working year of 300 shifts for all active mills rather than on practical capacity. Such a theoretical capacity in 1942 would have been 77 billion rather than 48 billion board feet. Normally, however, many small mills operate only part of the year. In some regions this is desirable because employment in these mills supplements farm employment.

Operators who have a good supply of timber are now in a favorable financial position. There is every indication of a sustained demand that will absorb as much lumber as the industry is likely to produce if prices are not too high. The market will, in general, be less selective than before the war—with respect to species, grades, and sizes. Such less desirable species as beech, the true firs, and hemlock, for example, will find a more profitable market. Some markets may be lost because of short supply and high lumber prices, but the relation of supply and demand will continue to favor the operators who own their own timber. On the other hand, those who do not own timber enough to meet their needs will find competition with other forest industries for stumpage more intense. Manufacturers of pulp and paper, veneer, cooperage, and other products are, to an ever increasing extent, obliged to obtain their raw material from the same sources as the lumber industry.

All these factors vindicate the foresight of progressive owners who undertook sustained-yield management a decade or more ago. The more favorable outlook is largely responsible for the increasing number of operators interested in good forest practice today. More than one-third of the land owned by lumber companies is now given some degree of planned forest management, and one-fourth of the cutting on lumber-company land is good or of high order,[22] by far the best showing being in the South.

The Pulp and Paper Industry

Pulp and paper manufacture ranks second to lumber among the timber industries. In 1944, according to Forest Service estimates, it employed 175,570 full-time equivalent workers and paid total wages of $316,600,000. Several facts concerning this industry may be emphasized: (1) There is an expanding market for its products; (2) it depends on foreign countries for a substantial part of its raw-material supply; (3) it has a high degree of internal integration, and (4) it has large plant investments.

The use of paper and paperboard in this country has expanded from 57 pounds per capita in 1899 to 119 pounds in 1919, 243 pounds in 1939, and 317 pounds in 1946. The peak has probably not been reached. Furthermore, new uses for wood pulp such as rayon, cellophane, photographic film, and plastics have increased the demand, and chemical research continues to find new uses.

The raw-material supply for paper and pulp

products is complex (fig. 17). Imports come in at all stages—as pulpwood, wood pulp, and paper and paperboard—and reuse of paper adds substantially to the domestic supply of raw material.

The five standard pulp-making processes differ in wood requirements, yields, and products. Forty-five percent of the 10-million-ton pulp output in 1944 was produced by the sulfate process. Almost any species can be used for sulfate pulp; but most of it is made from southern yellow pine. The yield is less than half the wood weight. Sulfate pulp is used principally for wrapping and bag papers and paperboard. However, bleaching makes it suitable also for newsprint and higher grades of paper.

Twenty-four percent of the 1944 output was by the sulfite process, which is used for the best grades of paper, rayon, cellophane, and other pure cellulose products. Long-fibered nonresinous conifers —the spruces, balsam firs, and hemlock—are the chief species used and the yield is about 50 percent. This is the chief chemical process in both the North and the West.

Mechanical or ground-wood pulp, the major component of newsprint paper, and the most exacting in its requirements, accounted for 15 percent of the 1944 output. Only the long-fibered light-colored spruces, balsam firs, and western hemlock are suitable for this process, but the yield is about 90 percent by weight. Most of the ground-wood output is in the North.

The soda process accounted for only 4 percent of the 1944 output. It is used for pulping hardwood species, chiefly aspen and cottonwood in the North, and the yield is about 50 percent. Mixed with sulfite pulp, it is used for book and magazine paper.

The semichemical processes, accounting for 5 percent of the output, use almost any hardwood. The yield is 70 to 80 percent, and the principal product is corrugated board.

In addition to the standard pulp-making processes, the production of defibrated, exploded, and asplund fiber for manufacturing building board, insulating board, other fiber boards, and roofing is growing into a substantial industry—accounting for 6 percent of total pulp output in 1944. Using a wide variety of both conifers and hardwoods, these new processes hold promise for all forest regions.

The pulp and paper industry is compact. In contrast to the thousands of sawmills, there were

[22] See fig. 15, p. 48.

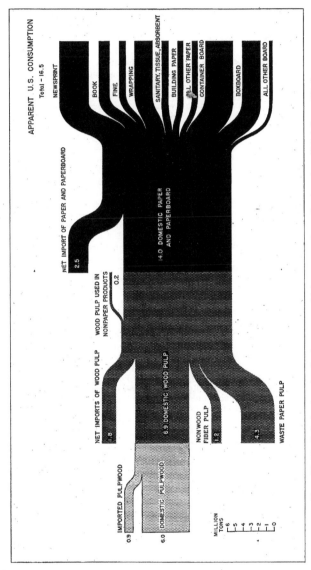

APPARENT U.S. CONSUMPTION
Total - 16.5

NEWSPRINT

BOOK

FINE

WRAPPING

SANITARY, TISSUE, ABSORBENT

BUILDING PAPER

ALL OTHER PAPER

CONTAINER BOARD

BOXBOARD

ALL OTHER BOARD

NET IMPORT OF PAPER AND PAPERBOARD
2.5

14.0 DOMESTIC PAPER AND PAPERBOARD

WOOD PULP USED IN NONPAPER PRODUCTS
0.2

NET IMPORTS OF WOOD PULP
1.8

6.9 DOMESTIC WOOD PULP

NONWOOD FIBER PULP
1.2

WASTE PAPER PULP
4.3

IMPORTED PULPWOOD
0.9

6.0 DOMESTIC PULPWOOD

MILLION TONS
6
5
4
3
2
1
0

FIGURE 17.—*The flow of pulpwood and other raw material into paper and paperboard products, United States, 1939 (in terms of million tons of wood pulp).*

only 237 active pulp mills in the country in 1944, all but 25 integrated with paper mills. The mills are located chiefly near the Atlantic and Gulf seaboard, in the Lake States, and in the Douglas-fir subregion.

Unlike the lumber industry, the paper and pulp industry is running at full capacity. During 1946, production reached 110 percent of rated plant capacity, yet the demand for many paper products was not met. Newsprint paper, much of which is imported, was especially short.

The pulp and paper industry is perhaps the most stable of the timber industries. Before the war an integrated sulfite pulp and paper mill of economic size called for an investment of 3.5 to 4.0 million dollars. For kraft pulp and paper minimum investment was 7 to 8 million dollars. Since such mills require a long amortization period, an assured wood supply becomes doubly important.

The industry owned about 15 million acres of forest land in 1944. This acreage is increasing, but few companies own enough to supply all their needs. Many pulp manufacturers have Canadian affiliates and own timber in that country, some of it acquired expressly for supplying plants in the United States.

Pulp and paper companies have been in the forefront of private owners in adopting forestry practices. More than two-thirds of the industry's lands is under management. In 1945, 33 percent of the cutting on pulp-company lands was "good" or "high-order"; another 49 percent was rated "fair." Only 18 percent was poor or destructive.[23]

Although the pulp and paper industry has adopted aggressive policies in forest-land acquisition, made a good beginning in forest management, and kept alert to improvements in technical processes of manufacture, its wood-supply problems are by no means solved.

Wood supply is a critical problem for many of the mills in New England and New York. Spruce and fir are in especial demand. Much of the supply comes from Canada. In New York some operators go into the woods for as little as 3 cords per acre. Premature clear-cutting of pulpwood timber is a common practice and this works against a shift to partial cutting methods which would give greater stability in the long run by maintaining productive growing stock.

In the Lake States, depletion of the preferred pulpwood species is even more advanced. Most of

the spruce and fir comes from Canada, and high-level production is being maintained by the increased use of jack pine, aspen, eastern hemlock, and hardwoods. Some spruce is now being obtained from Colorado, and lodgepole pine is shipped in from Montana.

The South now produces almost one-half of the Nation's total pulp output. The industry has expanded phenomenally there during the past 15 years. In some localities where new mills are planned, it is questionable whether the larger needs for wood can be met. Although most of the southern pulp and paper companies are managing their own timberlands well, nearly one-half of the industry's wood supply comes from other lands, where growing stock is being depleted by heavy cutting of small second growth.

In the Pacific Northwest, the dominant sulfite mills have already expanded close to the limits of the supply of the favored species—western hemlock and Sitka spruce. There are, however, large volumes of balsam firs, Engelmann spruce, and mountain hemlock farther up in the mountains which have been little used. With more hemlock going into lumber and plywood, sulfite pulp manufacturers have been actively expanding their timberland holdings. Further growth of the industry will doubtless be chiefly in the use of Douglas-fir for sulfate pulp. A large volume of low-quality logs and logging waste is available for such use.

Part of the deficiency in our domestic pulpwood supply may eventually be met by building pulp and paper plants in Alaska. The coastal forests, predominantly western hemlock and Sitka spruce, are well suited for paper making and could supply 1.5 million cords of pulpwood annually. This would be about 7 percent of our potential requirements.

Methods of procuring pulpwood vary. Much is purchased from farmers or independent loggers, often through brokers working in assigned districts. In such buying, the pulp and paper industry is generally able to outbid the lumber industry. Some of the wood is obtained from other timber industries. Imports from Canada are substantial in both the North and the Pacific Northwest.

Dependence upon contract buyers, who have little interest in either the permanence of the manufacturing plant or the continued productivity of the forest, is a disturbing element in the South and North. Possibilities exist for the creation, at strategic locations, of open pulpwood markets or timber-products exchanges where producers and

[23] See fig. 15, p. 48.

in sawlog operations or in lumber manufacture. Integrating the production of a combination of products, the specifications of which represent a progression in size and quality, should be profitable for small timberland owners, should reduce wood costs in the pulp industry, and should save timber.

The Veneer and Plywood Industry

The veneer and plywood industry has grown rapidly in the past 25 years. Its employment in 1944 is estimated as the equivalent of 54,170 full-time workers. Although it consumed only 6 percent as much timber as the lumber industry, and 30 percent as much as the pulp and paper industry, these figures do not measure its potential importance.

The industry has three main types of products: (1) Face veneers, made chiefly from high-quality hardwoods and used in furniture, cabinetmaking, paneling, and similar manufactures; (2) container veneers, made from southern pine, ponderosa pine, sweetgum, tupelo, birch, beech, maple, elm, cottonwood, etc., and used for orange and egg crates, baskets, hampers, and boxes for shipping fruits, vegetables, and other commodities, and crating for refrigerators, radios, etc.; and (3) plywood, made chiefly from Douglas-fir, and used for construction, door panels and other millwork, small boats, refrigerator cars, and hundreds of other purposes. New waterproof glues, improved methods of bonding, and the process of molding into various curved shapes have added greatly to the utility of plywood. In almost all its major construction uses, plywood is interchangeable with lumber and has several advantages. It can be produced in large sheets free of knots and other defects and can often be put into place with less labor.

Of the 1.5 billion board feet, log scale, used for veneer and plywood in 1944, 58 percent was hardwood and 42 percent softwood. Over half the total production of hardwood veneer was for containers. Furniture veneer, although in great demand and bringing high prices, constitutes a small part of total production.

806034°—49—5

plants, 32 of them in the Pacific Northwest and 2 in California, all but a few large and modern. Total capacity is about 2,150 million square feet (⅜-inch, 3-ply basis), but peak production (1942) has been only 1,850 million square feet.

Large, good-quality logs used by the veneer and plywood industry are becoming scarce. There are current or imminent shortages of logs for face veneers in each of the important hardwood regions. The Central, Middle Atlantic, and Lake regions probably have less than 10 years' supply of high grade veneer stumpage, at present rate of cutting. Possibilities of expanding the face-veneer industry in other regions are small. Container veneer, however, has less exacting requirements and there is enough hardwood to maintain the current level of production.

The hardwood plants buy logs from every available source—lumber manufacturers, independent loggers, farmers, importers (about 20 percent of face veneer). Attractive prices can be offered and logs can be transported long distances. Buyers for the larger concerns scour the country, purchases usually being made in small lots. High-quality face-veneer stumpage is often purchased as individual trees.

The softwood plywood industry of the Pacific Northwest is little more than two decades old. Yet there is an acute shortage of peeler logs in the Puget Sound, Grays Harbor, Columbia River, and northern Oregon coast areas, which had about 75 percent of the total installed capacity in 1942. The industry must adapt itself to new conditions.

Procurement of peeler logs for softwood plywood was almost exclusively in the open market until about a decade ago. Between 1937 and 1942 softwood plywood production more than doubled, while open-market supplies of all grades of logs decreased sharply. By 1944, only one-fourth of the industry's requirements was being drawn from log markets. Many good peeler logs now go into lumber.

The softwood plywood industry does not own enough timber to maintain production. It still relies largely on other owners because the high-grade logs and bolts it uses represent so small a part of the timber stand that investment in timberlands would be out of proportion to the size of the business. Plants are generally located in communities with sawmills, but it would be desirable to go further in integrating log procurement with that of the lumber industry.

However, to maintain output the Douglas-fir plywood industry will have to use lower-quality logs, and this will cause more direct competition between plywood and lumber mills for log supplies. It will also require more economy in the industry —use of poor-quality material for cores and backs, and patching of defective veneers. Since this inevitably means higher operating costs and lower quality of product, the plywood industry's competitive advantage in the market for high-quality logs will gradually be reduced. Nevertheless, there will doubtless be opportunities for new veneer mills in localities where the timber is still to be opened up.

There is not much prospect of expanding output by greater use of less desirable species of timber in other regions. Difficulties in drying and sanding, and the tendency to checking and glue staining, restrict the use of western hemlock and noble fir. The generally coarse and defective Douglas-fir in eastern Oregon, eastern Washington, California, and the Rocky Mountain regions is not suitable for plywood under present standards. The white fir of California is also apt to be highly defective. California red fir holds some promise but will also be used for lumber. The use of ponderosa pine and sugar pine for veneer might be expanded, but again this would run into competition with the lumber industry.

Other Timber Industries

Space permits only brief reference to other timber industries. Some of these illustrate critical situations arising from shortages of timber of the species or quality required. Others, although small in total output, may be valuable links in local integration for more effective use of timber in the woods and mill. Still others may furnish new employment and income in communities that lose major timber industries.

The output of the wood shingle industry is declining. This industry is based almost entirely on western redcedar and is concentrated in a few localities in the Douglas-fir subregion. The output of 3.4 million squares in 1944 was only one-third of the peak production about 35 years ago. The capacity of installed machines is about 12 million squares. About 25 percent of the wood shingles used in this country come from British Columbia. Because cedar occurs as scattered trees, the industry depends upon purchased stumpage except where affiliated with sawmills. With the passing of open log markets, many mills have difficulty in obtaining logs. The industry faces increasing competition from asphalt roofing and its future is doubtful. Of passing interest is the fact that defibrated wood is being used increasingly as base for asphalt roofing.

The tight cooperage industry is declining because of depletion of suitable timber. Most of this industry is in the Southeast, West Gulf, and Central regions. Suitable white oak, the chief species used, commands fantastic prices and waste is very great.

There is no shortage of raw material for the slack cooperage industry, which is more widely scattered and uses many species, including pine, redgum, spruce, elm, and Douglas-fir.

Hewing of cross ties is wasteful and the range of tree sizes that can be used is narrow. Because timber of tie size is at the threshold of its most valuable growth, tie cutting usually impairs forest-growing stock. In the South, hewn ties are made chiefly of southern yellow pine and oak. In the West, lodgepole pine and Rocky Mountain Douglas-fir are the chief species for hewing. Hewn ties constitute only a small part of all ties used.

Cutting of round mine timbers usually destroys immature growing stock. It is largely confined to the Middle Atlantic and Central regions. Since there is wide latitude as to species and size, most of the need for mine timbers could be met from thinnings and improvement cuttings.

The pole industry now uses chiefly southern pine. Use of western redcedar has declined because of shortage of suitable timber. Lodgepole pine, available in large quantities, is being more widely used to supply rural-electrification needs.

Cutting of piling commonly takes the form of thinning, because of exacting specifications that bar small timber and admit only the straightest trees. Piling is cut chiefly from southern pine and Douglas-fir. Because it brings high prices, cutting for this product is usually very profitable to the timber owner.

The production of naval stores from the gum of longleaf and slash pine trees is important in the South. With proper management gum production may be effectively integrated with the

Miscellaneous Publication 668, U. S. Department of Agriculture

production of pulpwood and sawlogs. When so integrated it opens the way for more intensive forestry than might otherwise be possible by providing substantial additional income.

Timber Industries in General Handicapped by Waning Timber Supply

The foregoing review of the principal timber industries points to timber shortage as a major handicap to sustained output. Other factors—especially skilled labor and equipment shortages—influence the situation currently, but raw material is basic and the major forest industries are finding the procurement of suitable stumpage more difficult and costly than in earlier years.

Local shortages of timber suitable for the established industries are critical. They are not fully revealed by regional data on timber volume and growth. In many localities the timber industries have been based on certain favored species, making no use of, and often destroying, large volumes of intermingled less desirable species. Sometimes it has been possible to go back over the land to harvest the species formerly considered unmerchantable, but industries that depend for profitable operation on superior species such as western white pine in the Northern Rocky Mountain region or sugar and ponderosa pine in California, must discount estimates of total timber volume to allow for the species that they cannot market to advantage.

Exploitation of favored species in the past aggravates the raw-material problem now. The removal of the best trees of the choice species often leaves the land in possssion of a poor-quality stand dominated by low-value species. Such conditions are generally unfavorable for a new crop of the more valuable species. Thus poor-quality hardwoods have taken over large expanses of eastern forests that formerly supported valuable mixed timber. And high-grading is being practiced also in the mixed conifer types of the West.

The availability of raw materal for the timber industries is further limited by transportation factors. Half of our saw timber is in the West, yet many of the established industries there will have to close because they can no longer get enough timber. New roads must be built into undeveloped country to make much of the timber available.

Ability of established industries to get timber from new localities is sometimes limited by the inadequacy of the public highway system or restric-

tions imposed upon highway use. The bulk of the timber now moves to the mills by motor truck. In many localities the public highway system will not stand such heavy traffic, or the grades and curves make log hauling impracticable. To overcome such limitations, some western timber operators have constructed their own roads paralleling public highways. Where the highways must be used, license fees or laws regulating truck loads, speeds, etc., often varying from State to State, add to the cost of transporting both raw material and finished product.

Railroad freight charges also have an influence on raw-material supply. In general, other things being equal, the farther the raw material must be hauled the less the manufacturer can pay for it at the loading point. Consequently the margin for stumpage goes down as shortage of nearby timber forces a manufacturer to go farther afield. This encourages "high-grading," species discrimination, and other wasteful practices in woods operations which, as previously pointed out, adversely affect future timber supplies. Indirectly, freight charges in getting the manufactured product from mill to consuming markets also have a bearing on timber supply. While these tend to be passed on to the consumers, the more distant manufacturers must absorb freight differentials in order to compete with those more favorably situated. This limits how far they can go and what they can pay for raw materials in the same manner as freight or other transportation charges in getting the raw material to the mill.

Industries Not Geared to Permanent Timber Supply

The impact of timber shortage on the forest industries has just been considered. A complementary question is how the location and character of these industries have affected the timber resource.

Too much manufacturing capacity in certain localities has led to overcutting of tributary forests. There are numerous examples of this now in the Pacific Northwest. Grays Harbor, for example, had 35 active sawmills in 1941 capable of producing well over 1 billion board feet a year. The cut in 1941 was 810 million board feet, of which 650 million was Douglas-fir and redcedar. Yet the tributary forests could sustain a cut of only 206 million board feet of these species.

One fundamental reason for such lack of balance is that the timber industries in general have been organized on a liquidation basis. Only recently have a significant number of enterprises been planned for continuous operation. It was inevitable that competitive exploitation of the original timber without regard to the sustained-yield capacity of the forest would lead to an overconcentration of plants in locations such as Grays Harbor, Puget Sound, and the Columbia River which combined easy access to a large volume of high-quality timber with cheap transportation to major consuming markets.

Excess plant capacity remains a problem in the older regions. In both the North and South, thousands of small sawmills with far greater capacity than the forests can sustain are a constant threat to essential forest growing stock and satisfactory forest management. Furthermore, New England, New York, and the Lake region have more pulp mills than their forests can support. Even in the South, concentration of pulp and paper mills at favorable points along the coast has led to rapid depletion of the local timber supply.

During recent years there has been a significant accumulation of forest land by manufacturers concerned about the future of their operations. Those needing more land frequently buy from those going out of business. Tax forfeiture of cut-over land has subsided. Yet lumber companies and pulp and paper manufacturers together own little more than one-tenth of all the commercial forest land. Obviously, much of their raw-material supply must come from other owners. In parts of the West, there is much interest in cooperative sustained-yield units whereby private forest land may be blocked up with adjacent government timber under a coordinated cutting plan. Such developments tend to strengthen ownership and give stability to a larger segment of the industrial timber supply. Acquisition of forest land by public agencies also works toward these ends.

Competition for stumpage aggravates timber depletion. Manufacturers who own enough land can plan on a permanent supply. Those who must depend on the purchase of stumpage are often forced to compete with one another. In many parts of the country the scarcity of stumpage has led to premature cutting of young stands. Furthermore, competition for stumpage has often resulted in liquidation of residual growing stock by owners who previously had undertaken partial cutting.

And because of this, operators who may strive to keep their own lands productive sometimes disregard future productivity when cutting purchased stumpage.

The small private holdings, including the farm woodlands, are in general suffering most from the scramble for stumpage. Yet an active demand for timber should be conducive to good forest practices on such lands. Farmers need to be shown that timber growing can be an integral part of their business and small owners, whether farmers or others, will often be better able to withstand pressure for destructive cutting if organized into cooperative associations through which output may be more effectively channeled into industrial use.

The adverse effects of competition for stumpage could be reduced in some sections by organizing timber-products exchanges. Experience with other commodity exchanges indicates that this would tend to assure the timber growers fair prices and good outlets, while the manufacturers would find a more dependable source of raw material.

Integration of wood requirements for various products should lead to more orderly timber use and better forestry. To put each cubic foot of wood to the highest use it can serve—high-grade logs into high-quality products, and low-grade material into pulpwood, fuel wood, or similar products—means a continual search for ways to eliminate waste and reduce costs. Integration within a single company may not always be feasible, but when it can be accomplished it usually results in more complete utilization and lower costs. For example, a combination of sawmill, pulp and paper plant, veneer mill, and chemical plants using wood and pulp-mill wastes may fit operating conditions in the Pacific Northwest. An outstanding example may be found in the integrated operations of one of the large companies at Longview, Wash.

Where plant integration is not feasible, the raw-material supply for independent sawmills, pulp mills, and specialty manufacturers may be integrated, as already suggested, through timber-products exchanges or by cooperative action among the manufacturers, the producers, or both. At any rate the presence of diversified timber industries in a given locality may afford ample opportunity to sell all kinds of timber to advantage. Such situations exist, for example, in southern New Hampshire and at Cloquet, Minn. They help make good forestry practicable.

In summary, the raw-material problems of the

Wood Waste

→>>> ──────────────────────────────── <<<←

Tightening of the raw-material situation in the timber industries throughout the country and acute shortages in many localities are focusing attention on wood waste. In this report "waste" is used in an intrinsic rather than an economic sense. Wood not used is classed as waste whether or not its utilization is now economically feasible.[24] The urgent need for lumber and the rapidly expanding market for pulp and paper provide powerful incentives for the reduction and use of waste in the woods. Better prices now make it possible to use material that formerly could not be handled at a profit. New uses for wood and improvement of manufacturing processes also open the way for more complete use of our timber. And making use of wood now wasted creates jobs that add to the economic welfare of timber-dependent communities. So it is well to consider the quantity and source of waste; its location and availability; how and to what extent it may be used; and how better use fits into a forest-conservation program.

Quantity, Source, and Location of Waste

An enormous amount of wood is wasted every year in converting trees into usable products. Only 43 percent by weight of the wood we cut, destroy in logging, or import appears in products other than fuel (fig. 18). Thirty-five percent is not used at all and the remaining 22 percent is used for fuel

[24] More specifically, waste refers to wood from the forest which does not appear in marketable products other than fuel. It does not include bark or byproducts like lath, shingles, pulpwood, wood flour, or baled shavings, or the volume of trees cut primarily for fuel; but it does include byproduct fuel-wood in woods and mill from trees cut for other products. Also included are losses of fiber, lignin, and other chemical substances in pulp processing. This discussion deals with waste in logging, manufacture of primary timber products, and remanufacture of lumber, but not with waste in other remanufacture or in use of products. Additional discussion and data are given in Reappraisal Report 4, Wood Waste in the United States. U. S. Dept. Agr., Forest Service. 1947.

—often very inefficiently. In 1944, wood waste was estimated at 108.9 million tons (table 22).

Logging waste accounted for 45 percent of the total, and only 7 percent of it was used for fuel. Most of the logging waste is in cut trees, but other trees destroyed during logging and slash disposal account for 12 percent of the waste in the woods. Some of the logging waste is suitable for lumber, especially in the Douglas-fir subregion.

Primary manufacture accounted for 49 percent of the waste in 1944. Almost half of this is in slabs, edgings, and other coarse material; another three-eighths is sawdust, shavings, and other fine material. The remainder (one-sixth) is fiber, lignin, and other chemical waste in pulp processing. In sharp contrast to the 7 percent of logging waste, 62 percent of the waste in primary manufacture is used for fuel. Some of this is sold for domestic use, but most of it is used in the plants where it originates.

TABLE 22.—*Wood waste, United States, 1944*

Nature of waste	Quantity	
	Million tons [1]	*Percent*
Logging:		
Parts of cut trees	43.3	40
Trees destroyed	5.7	5
Total	49.0	45
Primary manufacture:		
Slabs, edgings, and other coarse material	24.5	23
Sawdust, shavings, and other fine material	19.8	18
Lignin and other pulping waste	8.6	8
Total	52.9	49
Secondary manufacture of lumber	7.0	6
Total	108.9	100

[1] 2,000 pounds, oven-dry.

Waste in secondary manufacture of lumber is estimated at 6 percent of the total. All of this is presumed to be used for fuel. Although not included in this analysis, secondary losses of smaller

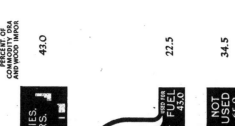
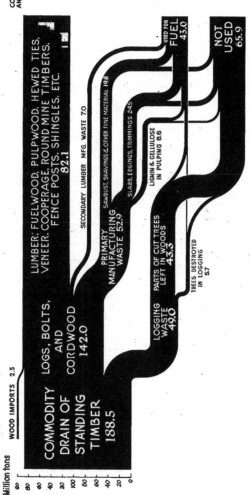

FIGURE 18.—*Use and waste in logging and manufacturing of all timber products, United States, 1944.*

volume occur in remanufacture of other products as, for example, when paper is made into bags and boxes.

Three-fourths of the volume of waste occurring in the form of wood arises in the production of lumber (table 23). Wood waste in pulp and paper making comes next, with about 5½ percent. (If to the waste as wood is added the fiber and chemical waste, the pulp and paper industry accounts for 13 percent of all waste.) Veneer and hewn cross ties each account for a little more than 4 percent of the waste volume, and the remaining 10 percent is divided among other products.

Manufacture of cooperage stock is the most wasteful of the timber industries: only 28 percent of the volume of the trees cut appears in the product. However, the total volume involved is small. Hewing of cross ties is almost as wasteful and accounts for twice as much waste, very little of which is used for fuel.

About two-thirds of the timber volume is wasted in the production of lumber and veneer. Little more than one-third of the lumber waste but almost half of the veneer waste is used as fuel.

TABLE 23.—Logging and primary manufacturing waste in relation to forest drain by principal timber products, United States, 1944

| Product | Forest drain | Waste | Proportion of drain | | |
			Used for fuel	Not used at all	Product
	Million cu. ft.	Million cu. ft.	Percent	Percent	Percent
Lumber	6,711	4,567	24	44	32
Pulp and paper [1]	1,306	325	8	17	75
Veneer	392	260	30	36	34
Hewn cross ties	363	254	4	66	30
Fuel wood	2,203	199	0	9	91
Cooperage stock	174	126	23	49	28
Fence posts and round mine timbers	445	47	1	9	90
Shingles	72	45	18	45	37
Other	516	192	17	20	63
All products	12,182	[1] 6,015	16	33	51

[1] Includes only waste as wood; excludes waste of fiber and chemical components in pulp and paper manufacture. Does not include waste from processing imported pulpwood, estimated at 9 million cubic feet.

Round products, like mine timbers, fence posts, and fuel wood, involve waste of only 9 or 10 percent, practically none of which gets used for fuel. In pulpwood operations, however, one-quarter of the wood is lost and, if chemical losses were in-

cluded, the percent of waste would be about the same as for lumber or veneer.

Only 20 percent of the waste is in the North; 44 percent is in the South and 36 percent in the West (table 24).

TABLE 24.—Logging and primary manufacturing waste by regions, 1944

Section and region	Logging waste	Primary manufacturing waste [1]	Total [1]
	Million cu. ft.	Million cu. ft.	Million cu. ft.
North:			
New England	130	103	233
Middle Atlantic	161	116	277
Lake	200	80	280
Central	293	116	409
Plains	4	3	7
Total	788	418	1,206
South:			
South Atlantic	297	393	690
Southeast	557	638	1,195
West Gulf	386	371	757
Total	1,240	1,402	2,642
West:			
Pacific Northwest	927	759	1,686
California	127	161	288
North Rocky Mtn.	59	98	157
South Rocky Mtn.	14	32	46
Total	1,127	1,050	2,177
United States	3,155	2,870	6,025

[1] Includes waste from both domestic and imported wood.

In both North and South the waste is widely scattered among thousands of small mills and a still larger number of small logging jobs. In the South the dispersion of logging waste is accentuated by the fact that so much of it arises from the cutting of light, understocked stands. On the other hand, primary manufacturing waste is somewhat more concentrated in the South than in the North because the output per plant averages much greater. The volume of mill waste in the South as in the North. Logging waste is much greater than primary manufacturing waste in the North because so much of the cut is from heavy-topped hardwoods.

Contrary to what might be expected, the volume of waste in the West is not as great as in the South, but because of the size of timber and character of the operation it is more concentrated. The greatest concentration is in the Pacific Northwest, where the bulk of the output is from large mills grouped around a few manufacturing centers. Logging waste assumes especially large proportions in the Douglas-fir subregion. Here clear-cutting of heavy

greatest accumulation of woods waste suitable for lumber or pulp anywhere in the country.

While the South already has a more diverse industry and makes fuller use of its forest crop than most of the West, it is significant that the proportion of all waste incident to lumbering is almost as great as in the Pacific Northwest. Because of the small size of timber being cut in the South, sawmill waste runs high and this tends to balance the heavy logging waste in the Pacific Northwest:

| Locality: | Waste as percent of lumbering drain in— | | |
	Logging	Milling	Both
South	29	39	68
Pacific Northwest	37	34	71

Conditions for waste-using industries are favorable in both the South and the West. Both have numerous localities where permanent primary manufacturing plants of substantial size can be sustained. Both need more industries to strengthen the local economy. The South needs new industries to absorb part of the labor force being released by changes in the acreage and technology of cotton production. The West needs them to employ part of a rapidly expanding population without increasing the drain on the resources, and to continue to support people in localities where forest depletion is forcing curtailment of primary timber industries. Because of the volume and concentration of both logging and manufacturing waste, the Pacific Northwest—the Douglas-fir subregion in particular—offers the most favorable opportunity. In the South the largest opportunity for industrial development based on use of wood waste is in the West Gulf region.

Possible Reduction and Use of Waste

It should be apparent from the foregoing discussion of the nature and distribution of waste that economic use of the entire volume disclosed by this study is impossible. There will inevitably be substantial quantities of small size, poor quality, or defective material left in the woods—especially in localities farthest from market and on terrain where logging is most difficult. Furthermore, it is unlikely that we will ever be able to gather up any large part of the waste from some 38,000 small sawmills; and much of the waste from the larger mills—especially those of medium size—will con-

every possible opportunity either to reduce waste or to use it.

Physical recovery.—Part of the waste in logging is simply the result of inefficient practices in felling and bucking. Waste in high stumps and from excessive or inefficient trimming allowance can be reduced by proper supervision or instruction and constant care. The amount of breakage and waste from poor choice of log lengths depends on the skill and judgment of the loggers. Waste from these sources is likely to be more important in farm woodlands and other small operations than on large operations where labor may be more skilled and supervision better.

More of the waste in logging may be recovered by the introduction of equipment especially designed to handle it. Great strides are being made in this direction in the Douglas-fir subregion. Widespread use of trucks and tractors instead of yarding engines and railroad transportation has given greater flexibility to operations and permitted the use of much material formerly left on the ground. The huge volume of material that cannot be economically handled by the heavy equipment still needed for logging the virgin timber often may be recovered by working over the area with light equipment either before or after the main logging job.

Portable sawmills are being successfully used to convert waste material on cut-over areas in the Douglas-fir subregion into rough lumber for shipment to finishing plants. Attention is also being given to portable chippers to convert material left in the woods, including that not suitable for lumber, to a form which will permit economic delivery to a pulp mill.

In the hardwood regions also, waste of material that cannot be economically handled in ordinary logging challenges our ingenuity to devise equipment and operating techniques to recover usable material in bolts or other form.

In many localities, integration of pulpwood cutting with lumber operations would help reduce logging waste.

There are similar possibilities for physical recovery of waste in primary manufacture. Inefficient practices, especially in the small mills which now cut so much of our lumber, cause much waste that can be eliminated by technical guidance and assistance. For example, inadequate power, poorly fitted saws, careless edging, and poor piling for seasoning are common causes of waste in small mills.

In the pulp and paper industry there seems to be room for improvement in facilities and practices for storage of pulpwood to reduce losses from decay while awaiting manufacture.

More facilities for manufacturing "small dimension stock" from hardwoods or "cut-up stock" from softwoods might increase the use of short lengths now wasted and permit recovery of more material from slabs and edgings. There are also possibilities of wider use of chips from trimmings, slabs, and edgings from the larger mills for pulp and paper manufacture.

Recent development of processes for shredding or defibrating wood for use in roofing, insulation, etc., has opened large possibilities for recovery of both logging and milling waste. This field of use holds particular interest because bark may be used along with the wood and because almost any species can be taken.

Not to be overlooked are possibilities for wider use of sawdust as filler in plastics and for insulation, wood flour, and other manufactures. The market for sawdust and shavings as bedding for cattle and litter for poultry may also be expanded.

Finally, the possibilities of profitable marketing of wood waste for fuel may be further developed. Briquetting of waste at large mills for domestic fuel has grown to large volume in recent years. The product is being shipped to all parts of the country and is apparently meeting favor with consumers. Wider use of wood waste might result from systematic efforts to increase convenience and reduce costs in the use of hogged waste, whether from mills or woods, for both industrial and domestic fuel.

Chemical recovery.—More dramatic in possibilities and in appeal to the imagination is the recovery of waste by chemical processes. However, the opportunities in this field appear to be limited. Profitable chemical recovery other than the manufacture of pulp and paper usually requires correlation with the lumber or other primary industry in order to keep the cost of raw material down. The prospect of direct recovery of logging waste for chemical manufacture other than pulp and paper is at present small.

In the pulp and paper industry the biggest opportunity lies in recovery of the waste in chemical pulping liquors. Since most of the waste in chemical pulping is lignin, losses may be reduced by modifying the processes so as to leave some of the lignin with the cellulose fiber. Some progress in this direction has been made in recent research.

Processes have also been developed for the manufacture of ethyl alcohol from sulfite pulp waste by fermentation. Widely used in Europe, this kind of recovery is now being applied on a commercial scale by one large plant in western Washington. Further possibilities in this field lie in the production of protein food for cattle (and potentially also for man) by the action of yeast or fungi.

Perhaps the chief opportunity for chemical utilization of sawmill waste lies in new processes of hydrolysis yielding sugar that can be fermented to produce ethyl alcohol, or used for growing of yeast protein. A commercial alcohol plant using wood waste must be so large that there are not many locations where an adequate supply of mill waste could be assured. One such plant has been erected near Eugene, Oreg. Success will depend in part on ability to recover byproducts, particularly those derived from lignin, which is the principal residue and now used only for fuel. Dry ice is a byproduct of the fermentation process.

Other possibilities of chemical recovery may be developed by partial hydrolysis yielding a plastic material that may be used as molding powder or converted into building boards. Furfural, a chemical needed in the plastics industry, may be obtained as a byproduct.

These illustrations of processes that appear ready for commercial application suggest other possibilities that may be developed as knowledge of wood chemistry grows.

Public aid.—The possibilities for waste reduction and use outlined above suggest public action in at least three lines to stimulate progress.

One that can have quick results in all parts of the country is more technical advice and assistance to timber owners and processors. Small owners and operators in particular need help in applying more efficient logging or milling practices that will reduce waste. On-the-ground demonstration, training, and guidance give best results in improvement of technical operations. Marketing assistance to small owners and encouragement of forest cooperatives should help find outlets for material that might otherwise go to waste. Such assistance should also lead to better forest management.

Basic to progress in use of waste is research. Because of the public interest in full use of the timber

mentary wood requirements pooling their timber holdings for joint operation or, in a more general way, by over-all planning in a community to achieve and maintain good balance between the timber industries and local timber supply.

Lack of good forest management is another aspect of excessive wood waste. So long as timber was plentiful and cheap there was little incentive for close utilization. But as timber becomes scarce and prices advance, landowners and operators become increasingly concerned about waste. And when they put their lands under sustained-yield management and become conscious of the costs of replacing productive growing stock, better use for the whole crop may make the difference between success or failure. Thus, while ability to make full use of what is cut improves the opportunity for sustained-yield management, planning for sustained yield is a powerful incentive for the reduction and use of waste.

Relation of Better Use to the Forest Situation

Current information on the waste problem for the country as a whole is so sketchy and so many rapidly changing factors are involved that quantitative estimates of the possible use of material now wasted are very difficult to make and would seem to have little significance. It is worth while, however, to consider the possibilities in general terms in relation to the Nation's needs in forestry.

When all is said and done, the output of sawn products that may come from waste is likely to be only a small percent of the total. Everywhere except in the Douglas-fir subregion, recovery of sawn products from waste will have to be based on such refinements as more care in log making, better practices in small mills, finding practical means of gathering and handling short bolts now left uncut, and expanding the recovery of small-dimension stock from hardwood sawmill waste. Only in the Douglas-fir subregion are there opportunities for new or distinct operations in the recovery of sawn products from logging waste. Even here recovery is likely to be confined to a few favorable localities where large concentrations of usable waste are easily accessible.

Somewhat better opportunity exists to augment the pulpwood supply by use of material now wasted. This can be achieved by better integration with lumber logging and sawmills and by relogging.

67

As in the case of sawn products, the Douglas-fir subregion has the greatest concentration of both logging and milling waste that may be used for pulp. But because there are only a few pulp mills in the Pacific Northwest and because most of them are located on navigable water, distance from the mills limits recovery of logging waste for pulp manufacture even more than for lumber. Many of the logging operations where waste is now accumulating are too far from the pulp mills to permit salvage for this purpose.

Notwithstanding a growing use of building board made from specially treated wood fiber, new uses based on chemical processes seem more likely to broaden the field of wood use than to replace staple products such as lumber, plywood, and pulp.

In the aggregate, then, use of material now wasted is not likely to result in a decisive reduction of the pressure on our forest growing stock. In the main, our output of staple forest products will continue to be met by direct drain upon the forest, and this demand is not likely to be greatly reduced by new uses for wood waste. Conversely, it seems probable that should the output of new products that do replace lumber and pulp rise to a level that would significantly affect the pattern of over-all consumption, it would become necessary to supplement recoverable waste by drawing directly upon the forest itself.

In any event the long-range growth goals discussed earlier in this report would not be much affected by what may be accomplished in use of waste. This is so not only because of the considerations outlined above, but also because the volume of *usable* waste will be much less when the virgin timber is gone. More will be scattered and more will be in small pieces, economically difficult to handle. Less will be suitable for sawn products.

The benefits to be gained in use of waste, therefore, lie only partly in helping to bridge the gap between present output and potential requirements. Even more important is the contribution that new uses can make to national welfare in other ways. New uses serve to expand employment per unit of forest growth. This is needed to support people and strengthen the regional economy where timber is a major resource and the primary timber industries are declining. Thus the use of waste can serve to help cushion the economic shock of forest depletion. It has special significance for the South, where added employment would help offset the decrease in manpower needed for growing and handling the cotton crop.

At the same time the use of waste should add incentive for better forestry. Use of waste removes or reduces fire hazard on cut-over areas and it implies a broader and better opportunity to improve forest growing stock by using inferior species and less desirable trees. Unfortunately the effect is often in the opposite direction: the opportunity for added income through closer utilization may lead to premature cutting and liquidation of needed growing stock. However, as previously stated, ability to utilize material now wasted may spell the difference between success and failure in planning sustained-yield operations.

Thus, entirely aside from making a direct contribution to the Nation's immediate need for timber products, better use of the timber we cut can have an important bearing on our progress in the widespread application of sustained-yield management that will be needed to achieve desirable growth goals. A good market for all kinds of forest-grown material is the key to intensive forestry, and use of waste should be a major objective in a comprehensive program of forestry for the Nation.

Nontimber Uses and Services of Forests

>>>——<

Bettering the timber situation is only one facet
: the many-sided task of making forests produce
lequately. They should be managed for water-
.ed protection. Also they should be improved
ıd efficiently used for livestock range, for wild-
:e propagation, and for recreation.

In general, what is done to assure the Nation's
ood supplies will enable the forests to yield more
other products and services. However, further-
g the nontimber contributions involves some
oblems that need additional attention, for they
e an integral part of the forestry job lying ahead.

Watershed Protection— A Prime Function of Forests

Water and soil not only sustain forests but are,
turn, profoundly affected by them. This in-
ıence extends far beyond forest land itself. Water
a product of most lands, and our 624 million
res of forests materially affect its disposition and
efulness. Moreover, forests are guardians of the
il, keeping it in place for productive purposes
ıd out of streams and water-storage works where
is harmful.

Water use and control have assumed great na-
ɔnal importance. One expression of this is the
ovement for regional development of natural
sources, which is spearheaded by the widespread
:mand for better use of water resources. Another
the magnitude of investments and projected
ɔrks to assure water supplies or to abate flood
ımage. There is growing recognition of the flood
enace. In 1936 this led to organic Federal legisla-
ɔn that includes broad authority for watershed
:atment in aid of flood control.

Cities and communities everywhere face difficult
oblems of water supply. The per capita use of
ıter in cities averages about 40 gallons a day.
.dustry uses huge quantities—3,600 gallons to
ake a ton of coke; up to a million gallons to
ake a ton of paper; and 70 gallons to make a

pound of finished woolens. Billions of dollar
invested in supply works and purification pl
It is a costly, relentless struggle to provide ar
dependable water supplies for growing comn
ties and industries.

Water from forest watersheds also finds ɑ
essential uses—for navigation, for hydroelɑ
power, for irrigation of more than 21 million
of arid cropland in the West. It lends charm
recreational value to the forest environment.
these uses are increasing and in the long run
have to be underwritten by good watershed
agement.

Destructive waters are of even more direct
cern. Floods and water-borne sediments, orig
ing in many instances on abused forest, range,
farm lands, are exacting a heavy toll. They ɑ
much human misery, loss of life, and about
million dollars property damage annually.
also impair the usefulness of thousands of
Nation's reservoirs which represent a total ca
investment of more than 4.5 billion dollars.

Watershed services in all parts of the cou
are below par. Forest fires are a major caus
unsatisfactory conditions. Overgrazing is also
.portant. It has damaged plant cover and soi
perhaps 20 percent of the forest land, especial
the West and North. In addition, sizable ɑ
have been cleared for various uses, for roadv
and for other types of construction.

Except in the virgin timberlands of the W
the greater part of the commercial forest acı
has been cut over—many areas several times.
practices which characterize more than half
timber cutting (see p. 46) are more than a tł
to sustained timber output. They are lea
their mark on watersheds as well.

The impact of all this is reflected in acceler
erosion, more damaging and more frequent flɑ
sedimentation, and impaired water supplies.
clear that forest programs and management ţ
should give more attention to watershed asţ

Watershed protection, like timber growing, is best served when forest soils are kept stable and productive. Mainly this involves the elimination of destructive logging and overgrazing, protection against fire and other hazards, and the rehabilitation of devastated or sparsely stocked forest lands, including some of the low-grade noncommercial types. Good forest practices—still far from general attainment—will go a long way toward providing satisfactory watershed conditions on the great bulk of the commercial forest lands.

But under certain conditions, some practices need to be supplemented or modified in the interests of good watershed management. Fire-protection plans should give more recognition to high-risk or special-value watershed areas (see pp. 81, 84). How to lessen disturbances to ground cover and soil in logging operations also needs constructive attention. In some areas the generally acceptable cutting practices may need modification to afford more protection or to increase water yields. Local situations of this kind occur on steep slopes, frozen soils, or in areas of rapid snow-melts such as the White Mountains of New Hampshire; on the unstable, highly erodible soils of the West and of the southern Piedmont and upper Coastal Plain; and in the rougher mountain sections, both East and West.

Good range management also helps provide good watershed conditions. But, as with timber management, practices which would aid recovery are not always applied. There is constant pressure to overstock and the range is often grazed too closely. Livestock are trailed where they should be hauled. These and other practices which are detrimental must be corrected. Deterioration from past abuse is so great on critical areas of the western forest range that it will take many years of careful management to attain satisfactory watershed conditions. Some forest land on steep slopes with easily disturbed soils should be closed because grazing it is virtually impossible without endangering watershed values.

Watershed improvement is beset with many difficulties. Public apathy and lack of understanding is a potent obstacle. For the most part, people are unaware of serious watershed situations even after floods or other calamities occur. Little is done about them because the public does not understand the cause or the cure or is not sufficiently aroused to demand action.

Inadequate technical knowledge also hampers watershed protection. There have been some notable research contributions but as yet they have not come into general application. Land managers have much to learn about how timber cutting, grazing, and other uses may be harmonized with watershed services. They need more information on how forest and range practices affect water and soil. They need a working knowledge of the economics of watershed management, and techniques for maintaining water supplies, stabilizing soil, and controlling runoff. It will take greatly strengthened research to provide all this.

Watershed management is preeminently a public responsibility and public forests afford the main opportunity for it. Many lands of high watershed value are in Federal, State, and community ownership—notably the national forests. Their management should set the pattern for all watershed lands. However, several things stand in the way of putting them in first-rate shape for watershed protection.

Many public forests are remote. Some are poorly consolidated and hence difficult to manage. Much of the land, severely exploited before it was placed under administration, is difficult and costly to rehabilitate. Whatever the obstacles, it will take intensified protection and management and a great deal of watershed restoration to assure satisfactory watershed services. Mostly this is a matter of more adequate facilities to do the work.

Public forests should be extended to include many millions of acres of critical watershed lands not suited to private management. Private owners have little incentive in watershed management, since it yields no direct revenue and mainly benefits others. Furthermore, the high cost of restoring badly depleted watershed lands usually precludes private investment. The job clearly will have to be shouldered mainly by public agencies.

Yet there remains the hard problem of assuring reasonably good management, in the public interest, of watershed lands in private ownership. At present these include about two-thirds of the lands having major or moderate protective influence.[25] Most of the unsatisfactory watershed conditions center here. Bettering them is closely linked with getting good private timber management, though it is inherently more difficult. There are no pat solutions, but basic remedies generally lie in fostering good cutting practices and con-

[25] See p. 15.

animals. This has great economic value to rural people, and provides opportunity for badly needed diversification of agriculture.

Forest range is currently in strong demand in all parts of the country. Indicative of this demand are the numbers of livestock, exclusive of dairy cows, in the 11 Western States—11.2 million cattle and 13.9 million stock sheep[26] in January, 1947. Even though there has been a moderate decline in cattle numbers and a material decline in sheep since the peak during World War II, the western range livestock population expressed in animal units is 10 percent above the average of the four prosperous years 1926–29 and 5 percent above the 4-year period preceding World War II (fig. 19). Recent declines in numbers, while favorable, are not sufficient to relieve western forest ranges of rather general heavy grazing. In seven Southern States cattle numbers have increased about 25 percent in the last 10 years. Elsewhere, there has been a similar upsurge followed by a moderate decline. Looking ahead, demand for livestock products is likely to continue high. This means that forest ranges will probably be under continuing pressure to carry as many livestock as possible.

Throughout much of the West there is widespread depletion of forest ranges. Most of the western ranges were fully stocked before 1900, and in many instances they were overgrazed and deteriorating. They deteriorated further as a result of too heavy stocking during World War I and again in the early and mid-thirties. Many have failed to recover. However, some in the national forests and well-managed private ranches have improved considerably over the years.

Although current data are meager, rough estimates indicate that about two-thirds of the western forest range is in unsatisfactory condition. The worst is the pinyon-juniper range, mostly in the arid Southwest; the least depleted is that of the open forest types, chiefly within national forests.

The hardwood forests east of the Plains have also been badly damaged by grazing; here, however, impairment of timber and watershed values is the main consideration. In many instances livestock should be excluded or greatly reduced in numbers. On the other hand, few of the pine forest ranges of the South are overgrazed.

Putting the Nation's forest ranges in good condition is an important aspect of the forestry job. First of all, deterioration of forage and other values

---

[26] Sheep other than those being fed for market.

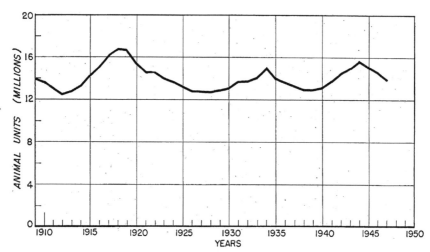

FIGURE 19.—*Cattle (dairy cows excluded) and stock sheep in 11 Western States, expressed in animal units (1 unit = 1 cow or 5 sheep), 1910–47.*

should be halted through elimination of overgrazing and other unsound practices. This is difficult because of the strong economic pressures to put more animals on a range than it will support. Secondly, millions of acres of badly depleted forest range that are producing only meager forage should be rehabilitated. In a larger sense grazing should be harmonized more effectively with other forest uses; and use of range and croplands should be better integrated for more efficient utilization of available forage.

Basically, this means that a better job of range management needs to be done on both public and private forest lands. More attention should be given to conservative grazing use that will build up and maintain the forage. This would include better seasonal use, more efficient control and distribution of livestock, adjustments in kinds and classes of animals using the range, and improved practices such as deferred and rotation grazing for speedier range recovery. It would call for large investments in water developments, fences, and other range improvements. But research has clearly shown that a reduction of livestock numbers and better management on overgrazed range will result in greater output of meat and larger calf crops because of better conditions for the animals

that remain. This usually means more profitable operations.

On the western national forests, progress in range improvement and adjusting livestock numbers to grazing capacity has been made since World War I. Range reseeding has been undertaken on a commercial scale in recent years. Yet about half of the range allotments still need adjustments, ranging from minor changes in management up to 50 percent reduction in numbers or even, in a few cases, total exclusion. In many instances small reductions made from time to time were insufficient to offset the range deterioration. And in some localities the reduction in livestock use has been partly or wholly offset by increases in big game.

Other Federal forest ranges in the West are in a similar although generally less satisfactory status. Constructive efforts to correct the severe overgrazing on public domain lands date mainly from 1935, when large areas in the West, including some 17 million acres of forest range, were placed under administration as grazing districts. Serious overgrazing prevails on many unreserved public domain lands, which are leased for grazing with few if any restrictions as to use. Some of these are forest range. On Indian lands, which include 12 million acres of forest range, there has been prog-

Miscellaneous Publication 668, U. S. Department of Agriculture

ress in recent years toward eliminating over-grazing; nevertheless, some of these are still deteriorating.

Keeping livestock in proper balance with forage and feed supplies is fundamental in range management. Without it, reseeding and other restorative measures accomplish little. Experience has shown that economic inducements to lower the rate of stocking often are not effective. Education and other publicly sponsored programs will help, but the solution to this basic problem rests very largely with range users and owners, who must gain greater understanding of the range and how to manage and use it properly.

Another important need is to unscramble the complicated ownership pattern which in many parts of the West seriously hampers management of forest ranges. Largely the result of earlier Government land-disposal policies, it typically presents a confusing array of small private holdings, State lands, alternate railroad grant sections, and speculative holdings, often interspersed with blocks of Federal land.

Many ranchers make part-time use of public range, some of them grazing lands administered by several agencies under differing policies and regulations. There is need for consolidation of ownership, where practicable, and for better coordination of public procedures and policies. On national forests and grazing districts, administration has been facilitated by transfer, leasing, and exchange of land. Much wider application of these procedures is needed.

Land is frequently a limiting factor in sound private ranch ownership. Ranching often requires 6,000 acres or more to provide a satisfactory living. The amount of land needed depends on such factors as its location and physical character, its capability for forage production, the development of improvements, and the kind of management it gets. Many western ranches are of an uneconomic size or poorly developed, and afford poor prospect for range conservation and betterment. Public aids, such as technical assistance, grants for range betterment, and sound credit on liberal terms, will help small ranchers meet this problem. But in some instances the only practical solution is outright public purchase.

Public forest ranges should serve as models of conservation and good husbandry. Yet range management on many public lands is still in its developmental stages, handicapped by limited fa-cilities. Even on the national-forest ranges, under administration and protection for several decades, there is need for intensified management to improve forage and livestock production. Generally this involves more men and money to do the management job. It also requires capital improvements on a large scale—reseeding depleted ranges, improving stock water supplies, eliminating noxious plants, and providing facilities such as fences and driveways.

More research is also needed. Only in the last 10 years has range research been extended, even on a limited scale, to all western regions and to the South. It has already done much and can do more in fostering range improvement and profitable livestock production.

Forest Recreation— A Large and Growing Use

Much of our outdoor recreation seeks a forest environment. People by the millions go to the forest to picnic or camp; to hunt, fish, or pursue other interests; or simply to enjoy the spaciousness, solitude, or scenic qualities of wooded country.

Most forest lands have potential recreation value. Perhaps two-thirds of the total acreage is actually available, in some degree, for recreation use.

Recreation in the last few decades has become a major forest use and a big business. At least half a million people earn all or part of their living supplying services, accommodations, or equipment to those who seek forest recreation.

Forest recreation especially benefits the countless small, back-country communities which derive much of their income from tourist business attracted, in large part, by the forest setting. For example, in Flathead County, Mont.—a typical forest county—recreation during its season affords more employment than logging and supports about one-tenth of the trade and service employment.

Large investments indicate the importance of forest recreation. On national forests about 27.5 million dollars of Federal funds has been spent on recreation improvements and some 37.5 million of private capital is invested in resorts, ski lifts, summer homes, and other facilities. Throughout the West, hundreds of dude ranches cater to forest visitors. In the East, particularly the mountain forests of the New England States, millions of dollars are invested in hotels, resorts, and other accommodations. Many commercial and civic organizations spend large sums to attract forest recreationists to their communities. These expenditures spell jobs for many rural people.

Recreation values on private forest lands are as yet far from fully utilized. Some of the private forests' in New England, the Lake States, the Appalachians, and other sections include superb scenic resources and support flourishing recreation industries. But a limiting factor is that recreational uses are mostly confined to those yielding the owner a money return.

Most people look to public forests for recreation. Of these, the national, State, and municipal parks are dedicated exclusively to recreation use. The national forests—of major importance by virtue of their size, distribution, and character—as well as most State and community forests, are administered under multiple-use policies that give due weight to recreation. In large part, management problems on all public lands are similar, but this discussion focuses on national-forest recreation, for which detailed information is at hand.

People enjoy many kinds of recreation on national forests (fig. 20).[27] In 1941, the peak year before the war, recreational areas received 10.75 million visits, and the other national-forest lands 7.5 million. Recreation uses, which fell off during the war, are now sharply on the upswing. They should about double in volume in the next 10 years (fig. 21).

National-forest recreation has generally developed without serious conflicts with other uses. Mainly this is because many forms of forest recreation—camping and picnicking, swimming, winter sports, and the like—though they involve exclusive use of the land, do not require a large acreage. In the aggregate these uses, present and potential, will require only about 300,000 acres—less than 1 percent of national-forest lands:

Class of area:	National forest lands reserved or needed for recreational use (1,000 acres)
Camp and picnic	44
Winter sports	77
Special uses	26
Total, 1945	147
Additional area needed, 1946-55	150
Total	297

[27] Charted data based on visitor's expressed reasons for visiting national forests; these data are not comparable with those in figure 21, which shows actual use of recreational areas.

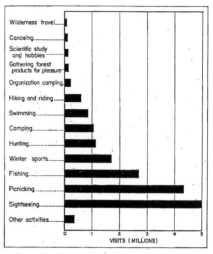

FIGURE 20.—*Primary purpose of national-forest visits, 1941.*

An additional 14 million acres is set aside as wilderness areas, but only about one-third is commercial forest, most of it remote and economically inoperable; and 1.5 million is reserved in roadside strips.

National-forest recreation facilities include some 4,200 camp and picnic grounds, 254 winter-sports areas, 201 swimming areas, and 54 organization camps. Before the war, these facilities were nearly meeting the demand and were in reasonably good shape, as a result of Civilian Conservation Corps work. They deteriorated greatly during the war for lack of maintenance. Even when fully restored, they probably will not match the growing demands which now tax available facilities to the utmost.

If the demand of the next 10 years on national forests is adequately met, the capacity of winter-sports areas and organization camps will need to be doubled, according to Forest Service estimates; and the area devoted to swimming, camping, and picnicking increased more than twofold.[28]

[28] Private facilities, which supplement and increase national-forest recreational use, include some 500 resorts, 300 organization camps, and about 13,000 summer homes constructed under special-use permit. Capacity of the resorts will perhaps have to be increased about two-thirds in the next 10 years to meet the demand.

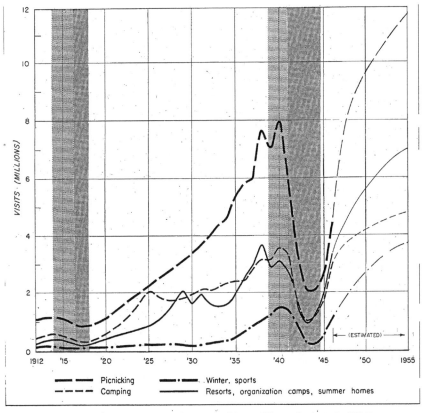

FIGURE 21.—*Trends in some recreational uses, national forests, 1912–46, and estimates for 1947–55.*

elk and moose, bighorn sheep, mountain goats, and bear—and roughly one-fourth of the lesser game and fur-bearers live in forested areas. Bird life abounds in most woodland. And forest-sheltered streams and lakes are the habitat of trout and many other fine game fish.

The public has a great and growing interest in forest wildlife. The main values are social and esthetic. But forest game also has real economic value.

For one thing, it supplies large quantities of food which supplements the American diet, particularly that of low-income rural people. In 1942 forest game supplied an estimated 104 million pounds of dressed meat and about 200 million pounds of fish, along with large quantities of fur and hides—all valued at about 150 million dollars.[29]

Moreover, sportsmen, who held some 21 million fishing and hunting licenses in 1946, spend a large sum annually on licenses, equipment, and services, much of it in taking fish and game in forest areas.

Most forest wildlife has persisted despite heavy slaughter and destructive forest practices. Fire, timber cutting, and forest clearing have greatly altered wildlife habitats—often adversely. Locally, some forms of wildlife have disappeared or have been pushed back with the receding old-growth timber. But generally, the more open, less extensive forests of today afford better food and cover than the original virgin stands. They can, however, be greatly improved for wildlife.

America's 215 million acres of public forests—the main areas to which people have ready access —puts about one-tenth of the total land at the disposal of the general public for hunting, fishing, and other wildlife uses. These widely distributed key areas should be proving grounds for new techniques of wildlife management, and serve to demonstrate them to private owners. However, public forests cannot wholly supply the demand for wildlife development.

The 409 million acres of private forest land could produce much more game than the public forests. Practical means should be found to foster wildlife on them.

As yet game management, even on public forests, has gone little beyond protection. Improvement of the forest habitat is a neglected phase which can often be accomplished as a part of other forest

uses and activities. Timber management is an especially important tool for improving game food and cover. For example, rather heavy selective cutting or clear cutting in blocks is, on the whole, beneficial since it increases the food supply, yet affords plenty of dense cover for escape and shelter. Timber-stand improvement and other measures also aid habitat improvement, if carried out with suitable regard for wildlife needs. Other forest uses, too—including grazing use by livestock—can be guided so as to complement and avoid conflict with wildlife management.

There are many reasons for slow progress in wildlife management. Some stem from the divided jurisdiction over land and game. Power to regulate hunting and fishing rests in the States whereas game management itself depends largely on the landowner. Without active landowner participation in wildlife programs there will be only incidental crops of fish and game to regulate. And few owners will attempt game management as long as they exercise only limited control of the harvest.

One reason why most private owners are little concerned with wildlife and are slow to adopt management is that game may damage timber or farm crops, and other values. Another is the increased forest-fire hazard and nuisance aspect of hunting and fishing. The small size of most private forest properties is an important deterrent. However, the major reason is lack of financial incentive. So far, States and sportsmen alike have resisted paying forest owners for hunting or fishing on their land.

Private owners should have more technical advice and assistance from public agencies in wildlife management. There is particular need to reach industrial forest owners more effectively and to do a better job of educating the general public on the value of wildlife and how to foster and harvest it. Financial returns, however, will do most to promote wildlife management in private forests.

Inadequate State game laws also hamper progress. Some involve a maze of local laws applicable to individual counties which all but defeat good game management. In some States, skilled administrators are lacking and in about 25 there is inadequate authority to administer wildlife resources. Frequently local courts are unwilling to enforce game laws.

Overstocking on both public and private lands,

---

[29] Forest Service estimates based, in some particulars, on reported statistics of the total take of meat and furs.

as in the case of domestic livestock, is another obstacle to good management. Usually this is the result of overprotection, which in some localities has built up game population far beyond the sustaining capacity of the forests. It engenders damage to farm crops, increases the competition for forage, and impairs watershed and recreational values. Correction of overstocking is difficult because of deeply rooted and often mistaken public sentiment for game protection. Public opinion with respect to game surpluses should be tempered by better understanding of wildlife needs and the limitations of the forest environment. Educational work, particularly among sportsmen, seems the most promising approach.

Insufficient technical knowledge also hampers wildlife management. There is not enough research on food and cover requirements and how to supply them. Much research has dealt with species injurious to forest or range—too little with problems of producing and harvesting wildlife crops. Although Federal agencies and the States will have to do most of this, the research facilities of universities, museums, and private organizations should be enlisted more effectively. Cooperative wildlife research units, now established in 13 States, need strengthening, and the program should be extended to many more States.

There is also a very important need to get capacity crops of game from public forest lands. To facilitate this, some public forests should be enlarged to include lands essential for wildlife management. This would open additional areas to the general public for hunting and fishing, especially east of the Plains where less than 1 acre per capita is available for such use. Some western national forests should be extended to include range badly needed to assure year-long feed for deer and elk.

The chief need, however, is more intensive management of public forests—which is the main way to get a greater contribution of all their products and services. In large part this is a matter of additional facilities to do a good wildlife-management job. But beyond that it involves more widespread adoption among public land-managing agencies of multiple-use management practices that seek not only to increase forest wildlife but also to utilize it effectively.

Forests Need Better Protection

→>>> ———————————————— <<<←

One important aim of the forestry job ahead should be to stop unnecessary forest destruction. As pointed out earlier, this depends in part on better cutting practices, and on more intelligent use of forests. But it also means waging an all-out war against major enemies—fire, insects, and disease.

These destroyers are a threat to all forest values. In varying degree they affect timber, water, forage, wildlife, and recreation, even the soil itself. Fire, for example, can wipe out timber growth, the accumulation of years, in a matter of minutes. And, in other less tangible ways, it can impair the forest—its beauty, usefulness, and capacity to perpetuate itself.

Every day, on the average, 475 fires sear the forests of the United States. They burn 25 million acres yearly, an area as large as the State of Virginia. They destroy small trees—tomorrow's timber—by the billions. Annually they send up in smoke over 850 million board feet of badly needed timber, enough to build 86,000 five-room homes.

The direct monetary loss sustained in 1946 was conservatively estimated at more than 32.5 million dollars. This does not include the enormous intangible and indirect damages to forests. Whatever the true losses, they represent an intolerable threat to forest abundance.

Even more destructive of timber is the host of insect pests and diseases that make unrelenting attacks on forests. The wood they destroy amounts to a huge drain: for the decade 1934–43, the estimated average yearly loss was 622 million cubic feet. This compares with about 460 million cubic feet destroyed by fire. Yet it measures only the more obvious destruction occurring for the most part in major epidemics.[30]

Much is being done to curb fire losses. Indeed, a great deal of the emphasis and effort in American forestry has centered on protection against fire. But control of forest insects and diseases has made far less headway.

The forest protection job is chiefly a public responsibility. Fire, insects, and disease respect no boundaries. They attack forests on a wide front. Organized, collective action is required to suppress them, and experience has shown that this is best provided through public auspices. The problem is analogous to fire-fighting services and other public safety measures required in cities.

Protection of the National Forests From Fire

Organized forest-fire control began with the establishment of the national forests in 1905. Following the great fires of 1910 which dramatized the need for better protection, the national forests have been gradually opened up with roads, trails, and telephone systems. An efficient detection and fire-fighting organization has been established. Equipment and facilities have been developed. And over the years, the policy of top-notch fire protection has won increasing public support.

Meanwhile, the fire-control job has expanded, chiefly because of the establishment of many new forest units in the eastern and southern States. The acreage protected, which had been close to 165 million acres between 1916 and 1930, has been around 184 million acres since 1941.[31] Expenditures for protection other than fire fighting, which did not reach 2.5 million dollars before the establishment of the Civilian Conservation Corps, were more than 6.5 million dollars, or about 3.6 cents per acre protected, from 1943 to 1945.

The new national forests have added much to the fire-protection work load. Some are poorly consolidated. Many are in regions where woods

[30] Of great economic importance, though not included in the forest insect and disease losses mentioned, is the decay in wood products to which both insects and disease contribute. Financially, such losses doubtless far exceed those in standing timber.

[31] This includes intermingled or adjacent lands in other ownership which receive protection.

g is an accepted tradition. The fire prob-
s also grown steadily in the West as recrea-
uses, timber cutting, and other activities
icteased.

Trends in frequency of forest fires reflect this
(fig. 22). The number of recorded fires per million acres under protection averaged around 30
from 1914–23. Since 1936 it has averaged about

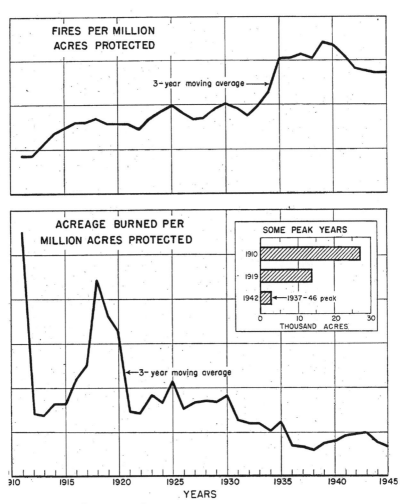

60, and exceeded 75 in 1936 and 1940. Although the fact is partly masked by the growing size of the job itself, fire control on national forests has become much more effective. The downward trend in acreage burned shows this (fig. 22). The average size of all fires 1937–46 was held below 25 acres, whereas for the decade 1921–30 it was 94 acres and for 1911–20, 174 acres.

Between 1933 and 1945 the Civilian Conservation Corps made available, for the first time, ample manpower and facilities for fire control. Termination of the CCC in 1941 left a gap which substantial military assistance and increased appropriations during the war did not wholly overcome.

It will be difficult to maintain the good record of the past 13 years. Equipment, badly depreciated during the war, is still below par. Costs have outrun appropriations. And rebuilding an adequate fire-control organization poses many problems. Partly offsetting the less favorable factors, however, are technological advances such as planes, parachutes, and other facilities which enable men to get quickly into remote mountain country and hit fires while they are small.

But how adequate is national-forest fire protection? Roughly indicative is the ratio of the average annual burn to protected area for a recent 5-year period (table 25). Of 184 million acres protected, an average of 317 thousand acres burned annually—a little over 0.17 percent. This is 29 percent more than in the prewar period, 1937–41, when abundant CCC assistance was at hand.

TABLE 25.—*Average annual burn on national forests, 1941–45, by major sections*

Section	Acreage under protection	Acreage burned annually	
	Thousand acres	*Thousand acres*	*Percent*
North	19,252	33	0.17
South	17,717	146	.82
West	146,978	138	.09
United States	183,947	317	.17

The area burned ranges from a negligible percent in New England to more than 1 percent in the South Atlantic and Southeast regions (fig. 23).

Undoubtedly, an over-all average annual burn of 0.20 percent or less is a good showing. It should not appreciably reduce timber yield, provided the damage is evenly distributed. However,

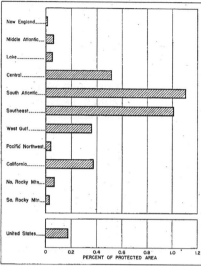

FIGURE 23.—*Average annual burn on national forests by regions, 1941–45.*

a low national rate of burn often obscures high rates of regional and local damage.

Even locally, a small average annual burn does not necessarily mean satisfactory fire protection. A large fire once in 25 years may not be tolerable even though the average burn remains small. And small fires may cause intolerable damage in critical high-value areas, such as the watershed lands adjoining Los Angeles and other California cities. In such situations adequate protection means virtual exclusion of fire.

Much the same applies to key timber-growing lands. Where recurring fires have converted much commercial forest to worthless chaparral—as in the California Sierras and the white pine type in northern Idaho—virtual elimination of fires may be required to conserve enough productive growing stock to sustain the local economy.

These and other variables make it difficult to generalize as to adequacy of national-forest fire protection. However, nearly all the commercial acreage is receiving good protection which, in every region, compares favorably with the best of that attained on forest lands in other ownerships.

On the debit side, there are many localities where a great deal of improvement is needed.

Rather generally in the South, the percent of burn is too high. In the North Rocky Mountain region, drought, lightning, and other factors combine about once every 5 years to set the stage for disastrous fires; here major effort will be required to keep the annual burn below one-tenth of 1 percent, the maximum amount consistent with satisfactory forest management for this region. Protection will need to be stepped up in many key areas in the Pacific Northwest. And in California, where timber, watershed, and recreation values are high and fires are unusually destructive, protection is clearly inadequate.

National-forest protection, then, should aim at: (1) Holding the annual burn on every working circle of commercial forest land to 0.20 percent of the area or less; (2) complete exclusion of fire from certain high-value areas, including critical watershed lands; (3) elimination of incendiary fires and reduction of man-caused fires to the accidental minimum; and (4) prevention of disaster fires—the big ones that get away.

Finally, forest-fire control effort and expenditures should be commensurate with national-forest values and the public benefits that accrue. New circumstances—such as the increased air travel into wild country, the opening up of remote areas to timber cutting, and the constantly changing public attitudes and demands—may profoundly affect forest-fire control on the national forests. We look increasingly to national forests for timber and other benefits. Their values are growing. Reflecting this is the trend in revenues from them, which have more than tripled since 1940. Wise public policy therefore calls for rising standards of fire protection, particularly for those key tracts that produce high income or other essential services.

Fire Protection on Other Federal Lands

Other Federal forest lands totaling about 54 million acres, of which 15 million is commercial, have a fire problem paralleling that of the national forests. They are administered by agencies of the Department of the Interior and are intermingled with some 121 million acres of wild nonforest lands also in need of protection.

About 54 percent of the forest land is in grazing districts, public domain, and Oregon and California revested grant lands administered by the Bureau of Land Management. Other categories include 16 million acres in Indian reservations;

7 million acres of national-park lands; and slightly less than 1 million acres held by the Bureau of Reclamation and the Fish and Wildlife Service.

Progress in fire control has been variable. Most forests in Indian reservations and national parks have been under protection for many years. The others have been brought under protection more recently. Fire protection on grazing-district lands dates from 1935, when they were placed under administration. For most of the lands the greatest progress has been since 1933 as a result of the Civilian Conservation Corps program.

Except for the Indian and the O&C holdings, these forest lands are administered primarily for purposes other than timber production. In the main, protection criteria have not been formulated by which to measure results.

Data for the several categories of land, 1941–45, are roughly indicative of protection accomplishments, although they apply to all lands under protection—predominantly nonforest lands (table 26). They show an average yearly burn of less than a million acres or about three-fifths of 1 percent of the 152 million acres under protection.

TABLE 26.—*Average annual burn on lands protected by the Department of the Interior, 1941–45* [1]

Administering Service	Area protected	Area burned	
	Million acres	*Thousand acres*	*Percent*
Grazing Service	99.4	758	0.76
Office of Indian Affairs	36.4	134	.37
National Park Service	9.6	12	.12
Fish and Wildlife Service	4.0	26	.65
O&C Administration	2.5	3	.12
Total	151.9	[2] 933	.61

[1] Exclusive of unreserved public domain lands for which data are incomplete; these lands are scattered and only partly under protection.

[2] Of the 776,000 acres burned annually from 1942 to 1945, only about 5 percent was forest land.

National-park and Oregon and California revested lands make the best showing, with an average annual burn of only a little more than one-tenth of 1 percent of the protected area. Grazing-district lands apparently receive the poorest protection, the average annual burn being about three-fourths of 1 percent for the 5-year period.[32]

Fire-control needs here aline closely with those on national forests. The objective for the Oregon

---

[32] The actual burn on forest lands may have been somewhat less in view of the greater fire hazard and lower standards of protection on the nonforest lands.

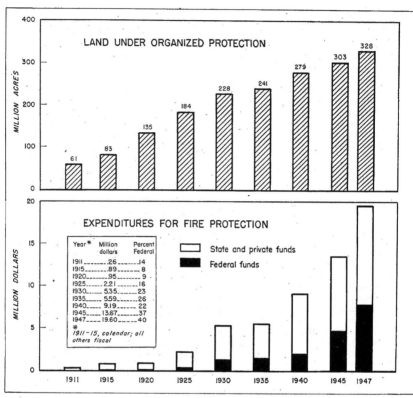

FIGURE 24.—*Area protected and expenditures, cooperative fire protection on private and State forest lands, 1911–47.*

and California revested lands and national-park lands—now receiving reasonably adequate protection—should be to maintain this good record and to intensify protection where needed for particularly critical areas. Both standards and accomplishments need to be raised substantially for the other four-fifths of these Federal forest lands.

Fire Protection on Private and State Lands

Organized fire protection on State and private forests got its first substantial impetus in 1911 through Federal support authorized by the Weeks Law. This Federal aid, restricted to forest watersheds of navigable streams, was broadened by the Clarke-McNary law in 1924 to apply to all timber lands as well as to critical nonforested watershed lands. These acts were milestones in cooperative fire control.

The area under protection increased steadily from 61 million acres in 1911 to 328 million acres in 1947 (fig. 24). Annual expenditures have risen from a quarter million dollars to more than 2½ million dollars in 1947, when they amounted to 6.7 cents per acre protected.

Federal appropriations for cooperative protection, consistently less than State and private ex-

Miscellaneous Publication 668, U. S. Department of Agricultur

area still burned over annually. And it must be kept in mind that protection has not yet been started on 27 percent of the State and private lands in need of it.

TABLE 27.—*Private and State forest lands without' organized fire protection, and annual burn*

Region	Without organized fire protection [1]	Annual burn [2]
	Million acres	*Percent*
Southeast	52	26
West Gulf	14	8
South Atlantic	4	1
Central	27	5
Plains (W. Okla. and W. Tex.)	13	19
North Rocky Mtn.	4	([3])
South Rocky Mtn.	6	([3])
United States	120	17

[1] Estimate for 1946.
[2] Average, 1941–45.
[3] No reliable data.

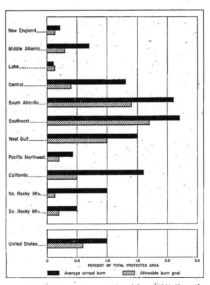

FIGURE 25.—*Relation of average annual burn, 1941-45, to the allowable burn, private and State forest lands under organized protection.*

The twofold job ahead, clearly, is to (1) bring unprotected areas under effective control, and (2) build up protection to reasonable adequacy where now spread too thin.

Unless progress is accelerated, it will take about 20 years to bring under protection the 120 million acres remaining in 1946. This is too slow. A reasonable aim would be to do it within the next decade. To many States, especially in the South, this is a major challenge.

For lands now under protection the allowable burn objective should be attained in all States as soon as possible. Except for critical watershed lands, these standards appear adequate for timber growing and the other uses of forest lands.

Topping the obstacles to satisfactory fire control is the man-caused fire. Ninety-seven percent of the forest fires are in this category and hence, in theory, preventable. Of the 68,000 which occurred annually, 1941–45, on protected private and State lands, more than half were caused by campers, debris burners, and the like, and 9 percent by railroads and lumbering (fig. 26). Twenty-eight percent were purposely set.

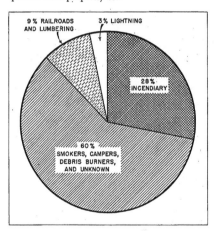

9% RAILROADS AND LUMBERING   3% LIGHTNING

28% INCENDIARY

60% SMOKERS, CAMPERS, DEBRIS BURNERS, AND UNKNOWN

FIGURE 26.—*Causes of forest fires, private and state lands, 1941–45.*

Incendiarism is most prevalent in the South, where it accounts for 43 percent of all fires. Here firing the woods is a long-established practice. When employed judiciously in certain types and under controlled conditions, fire can help estab-lish a new crop of pine, improve grazing, reduce the hazard from inflammable debris, and serve other purposes. But most of the woods-burning through-out the South is indiscriminate and seriously im-pairs forest values. It is also a troublesome local problem in some western forests.

Prevention of man-caused fires is a knotty prob-lem. Fundamentally it depends on an aroused public opinion. Effective educational work is being done by the Cooperative Forest Fire Preven-tion Campaign, and by the "Keep Green" and similar programs. Education on a much more ample scale is needed.

Paralleling the educational problem is that of obtaining satisfactory fire laws. In about one-third of the States, the laws are inadequate. Most of the States where protection is poorest—in the South, the Central region, and the South Rocky Mountain region—do not require brush-burning permits. Many lack other safeguards relating to slash dis-posal, campfires, and restricted use of forest areas during hazardous periods.

Better enforcement of fire laws is another wide-spread need. The quality of enforcement reflects the attitudes of the people and local courts. En-forcement has been weak in the Southeast and West Gulf regions.

Still another problem is finances. Costs have markedly increased, better information is avail-able on what adequate protection requires, and the area needing protection has been increased some 16 million acres. By recent estimates, adequate protection will cost about 40 million dollars a year, or more than double the estimate made in 1939. Total expenditures in 1947 were 22 million dollars. Obviously a dollar job cannot be done for 55 cents. Both Federal and State funds are short of the mark.

There is also need for more efficient adminis-tration—a responsibility of the States, primarily. There is wide variation in the efficiency of State forestry departments. This is related in one way or another to variations in value and extent of forest resources, in per capita wealth, in adequacy of fire laws, in civil service standards and salary levels, and many other factors. No uniform pat-tern or standards can be prescribed. Nevertheless, to achieve effective Nation-wide fire control, many State forestry departments must be further strength-ened so as to assure continuity of programs, able leadership, competent, well-trained staffs, and ample authority and money to do the job.

Epidemic losses are usually unpredictable. Little allowance can be made for them in the long-range management plans. Frequently so destructive as to jeopardize lumbering investments and operations, epidemic losses have always attracted most of the public attention and remedial action.

This country has many examples of damage from epidemics. The larch sawfly destroyed practically all mature stands of larch in the Lake States about 35 years ago. Chestnut was wiped out by an introduced parasite, the chestnut blight. Numerous bark-beetle outbreaks in the pine forests of the West and South have destroyed many billions of board feet of timber. Blister rust is a threat to valuable white pines wherever they occur.

Government agencies have mostly centered efforts on control of epidemics after they have become full-blown outbreaks; on quarantine and inspection to exclude foreign pests; and on research to develop the basic techniques of control.

Only a small beginning has been made in adjusting forest-management practices to reduce insect and disease losses. Yet, generally speaking, good forestry is the best preventive for these losses. It helps keep insects and diseases from reaching the epidemic stage where control may be very expensive, if not impossible. Moreover, well-managed forests are usually accessible and closely utilized. This permits better clean-up of dead and dying timber and greatly facilitates control operations. Conversion of natural stands to fast-growing, managed forests will remove the trees most susceptible to attack. A vigorous growing forest—a prime aim in forestry—suffers comparatively little injury from most insects and certain diseases. For others, against which mere vigor does not protect, much can be done through adjusting species mixture or stand density and avoiding unnecessary wounding.

During the decade 1936–45, 54 million dollars of Federal, State, and private funds was spent on control:

	Expenditures for forest insect-disease control, 1936-45 (million dollars)		
Item:	Federal	State and private	Total
White pine blister rust	26.2	2.5	28.7
Gypsy moth	12.9	11.0	23.9
Other insects	1.4	.1	1.5
Total	40.5	13.6	54.1

More than half was spent on white pine blister rust, about 44 percent on gypsy moth. Much of the latter, however, was spent for protection of

85

roadside and shade trees. The small expenditures for control of other forest insects—the bark beetles, weevils, defoliators, and other pests—reflect the national disregard for the heavy damage inflicted by them.

Federal expenditures exceeded 40 million dollars, about 75 percent of the total. A considerable part was spent on Federal forests. However, more Federal money was spent on private and State forest lands than the 13.5 million dollars from State and private sources. Most of the latter was for gypsy moth alone.

Emergency appropriations for the CCC, WPA, and other work-relief programs represented 54 percent of Federal expenditures for 1936-45 and about 45 percent of the total expenditures from all sources. Regular Federal appropriations increased from 1.3 million dollars in 1936 to nearly 3.1 million in 1945.

Control of insects and diseases has been too slow-paced. Valuable time has too often been lost while awaiting special Federal or State appropriations, or participation by private forest owners.

With this record of "too little and too late," the continuing threat of major insect and disease epidemics should be faced squarely. A widespread outbreak of spruce budworm now threatens spruce and balsam in the Northeast. The valuable commercial white pines may be confined by blister rust to areas of high productivity where expensive control can be economically justified. Destructive outbreaks of bark beetles and other major pests are hazards over wide areas. It will take fast, concerted action on a much more ample scale to keep losses to a tolerable level.

Clearly, several things have been lacking. Among them is a well-organized detection system to catch incipient outbreaks before they grow. With this, there should be adequate facilities for prompt suppression. Epidemics, like fires, almost invariably spread from small infestation centers. Discovering the trouble spots while they are small should not be left to chance. As in fire control, time is of the essence in both detection and suppression.

Not the least of obstacles is the deficiency of technical information on which to base control

action. There are many gaps in knowledge despite the effective work done in limited research.[36] For one thing, not enough is known about foreign pests. Machinery for preventing their entry is well developed. This, however, cannot operate as an efficient selective quarantine without more advance knowledge of potentially dangerous introductions.

Public agencies will have to lead the way in prevention and control. Indeed, as in forest-fire protection, the Federal-State responsibility is paramount. It rests, in general, on the huge public stake in forest resources; on the need for blanket application of control measures without respect to landownership or State lines; on the inability of individual owners acting alone to cope with these risks.

Control operations have demonstrated the need for concerted action—Federal, State, and private—particularly where forest lands of diverse ownership are intermingled. These activities need to be greatly stepped up. Private participation has been mostly by organized protective associations in the West. State participation has been limited. A primary need is for Federal leadership and participation at least on a par with that provided in cooperative fire control.

The Forest Pest Control Act of June 25, 1947, marks a notable advance toward meeting this need. It recognizes the Federal responsibility in Nation-wide forest protection against insects and diseases and provides flexible authority for direct action and for cooperation with State and other agencies. It sets the stage for an adequate system to detect incipient outbreaks and suppress them promptly.

On the whole, the protection of forests—whether against bugs, decay, or fire—is of high priority, and we need to get on with it without delay. There is widespread acceptance of the need for eliminating these hazards. There is also reasonable agreement on how to do it. Moreover, it is an essential phase of the much larger problem of getting good forestry practiced on private lands.

[36] Research expenditures, 1936-45, totaled only 3.8 million dollars—mostly Federal.

How Forest Ownership Affects the Outlook

Many aspects of the forest situation have been discussed, with particular emphasis on timber supplies. Attention now needs to be directed more sharply to the broad problems that are associated with ownership.

Character of ownership largely determines the treatment and management of forests, the stability of forestry enterprises, and the kind of action needed to put the Nation's forests on a permanently productive basis. It is therefore a fundamental factor in the forest situation.

Private ownership, which accounts for two-thirds of all forest land and three-fourths of the commercial, as shown in the following tabulation and figure 27, is of necessity motivated mainly by financial return.

	Ownership of forest land (million acres)		
Class of land:	All owners	Private	Public
Commercial	461	345	116
Noncommercial	163	64	99
Total	624	409	215

Private forestry as a rule must yield revenue commensurate with costs and without long waiting. It therefore centers on those uses, principally timber growing, that produce cash returns.

The need for large-scale public ownership—Federal, State, and local—has largely grown out of limitations that make good management in private ownership uncertain. One of these is the long-deferred or sometimes very small returns from timber crops. Another is the lack of incentive in bettering watershed protection and other services of the forest. Government ownership is relatively free of pressures for immediate revenues. Full recognition can be given to all forest uses and services including those which benefit the general public rather than the individual owner. Public ownership generally affords more assurance of continuity of policies and conservation practices than private ownership. It offers the best opportunity for multiple-use management and for the rehabilitation of forest lands where values are low or are slow to accrue. However, a very large acreage is economically suitable for private forestry.

This basic difference between public and private ownership bears importantly on both the handicaps and opportunities in forestry. But there are also differences among private owners and among the main public categories with respect to purpose, tenure, and stability, and facilities for practicing good forestry.

Administration:	Publicly owned or managed forest lands, 1945 (million acres)		
	All forest	Commer- cial	Noncom- mercial
National forest	123	73	50
Other Federal	54	16	38
State	28	18	10
Local government	10	9	1
All public	215	116	99

Nearly half of this, however, is noncommercial—the dry-site, scrubby, or reserved forests not suited or available for growing commercial timber though valuable for watershed and other purposes. About four-fifths is Federal (fig. 28), the national forests being the largest category.

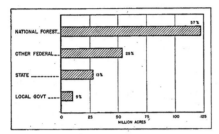

FIGURE 28.—*Ownership of the 215 million acres of public forest lands.*

National Forests—A Big Undertaking

The national forests, which today stand as the world's greatest public-forest system, include about 180 million acres (net) located in 40 States, Alaska, and Puerto Rico. About 159 million acres of this land is in the United States proper (table 28).

TABLE 28.—*Gross and net area in national forests as of June 30, 1946* [1]

Location	Gross acreage within estab- lished units	Net acreage federally owned and under Forest Service administration	
		All lands	Forest lands
	Million acres	*Million acres*	*Million acres*
United States	207.41	158.65	123
Alaska	20.88	20.85	[a]12
Total	228.29	179.50	135

[1] Exclusive of Puerto Rico units which include 186,000 acres, gross, of which about 31,000 is federally owned and ad-ministered.
[a] Rough estimate.

Withdrawals of forest land from the western public domain began in 1891. Six years later these forest reserves were put under administration, and in 1905 jurisdiction was transferred to the Department of Agriculture. In 1907 their name was changed to national forests, as more descriptive of their real character. The Weeks Law (1911) provided the first authority for purchase of lands, and made possible the establishment of national forests in the East. In 1922 a general exchange law authorized exchange of public land or timber for private land.

Of the 123 million acres of forest land in the national forests of the United States proper, about 100 million were withdrawn from the public domain. Some 18 million have been purchased; less than 4 million have been acquired through exchange, and about 1 million have been private gifts or transfers from other Federal agencies.

National forests are managed under four cardinal principles. First is the objective of the public good: "the greatest good to the greatest number of people in the long run." Second is the conservation objective: full and wise use of the forests so as to build up and perpetuate them. Third is multiple use: integrated management of all resources—timber, water, range, recreation, and wildlife—for maximum public benefits. Fourth is decentralized administration: the aim of providing on-the-ground administration in close and constant touch with local, State, and regional conditions and with only enough centralized control to assure that basic policies are effectively carried out.

Placing national-forest lands—in the aggregate about one-twelfth of our total land area—under intensive administration and management has been hampered by the remoteness and inaccessibility of much of the land, by poorly consolidated ownership in many instances, and by inadequate funds. Yet steady progress has been made. Timber, range, water, and other resources are being husbanded through protection, controlled cutting or regulated use, planting and reseeding, and other measures. A basic aim is to bring output up to the full sustained-yield capacity of the land.

Progress would perhaps seem larger if today's needs to get a maximum contribution from national forests were less pressing. As this report emphasizes earlier, the steady depletion of private timber has left the national forests, which include 16 percent of the commercial forest, with nearly a third of the Nation's saw timber. Prior to 1940, much of this

tions, 1910–46, ranged from 75 thousand to 3 million dollars annually.[38] In addition, about 48 million of emergency funds was made available for acquisition from 1934 to 1937. About half of the 18 million acres purchased to date was acquired in those 4 years.

The national forests are a great public asset capable of a much larger sustained output of timber and other products if more intensively managed. They are the backlog of America's public-forest holdings, destined to contribute increasingly to local and national economy. A most pressing need is to get a maximum contribution from them consistent with sound conservation principles. We can do this only by investing more in this resource.

Other Public Forests Are Also Important

The 92 million acres of other public-forest lands also have a large potential for furthering community and national welfare and, in some respects, have similar management problems. Some 10 or more agencies manage the 54 million acres in Federal jurisdiction, most of which is under the Department of the Interior:

	Federally owned or administered forest lands other than national forests [1] (million acres)		
	All forest	Commercial	Noncommercial
Classification:			
Grazing districts	17.0	1.0	16.0
Indian lands	16.4	6.6	9.8
Other Federal	[2] 20.3	7.8	12.5
Total	53.7	15.4	38.3

[1] Approximate data for 1945.

[2] Includes about 9 million acres in public domain; 7 million in national parks and monuments; 2 million in Oregon and California revested lands; and 2 million administered by other agencies, including the Reclamation Service, Fish and Wildlife Service, Soil Conservation Service, and the military departments.

The 17 million acres in grazing districts and 9 million in the unreserved public domain—all in the West and administered by the Interior Department's Bureau of Land Management—is mostly noncommercial and of value chiefly for range and watershed protection. Mainly these are arid forest lands intermingled with or merging into open range. Fire protection has been sporadic and management has gone little beyond initial attempts to better the range.

---

[38] No appropriations were made in 1916, 1918, 1919, and 1921.

The Oregon and California Railroad and Coos Bay revested lands, about 2 million acres administered by the same bureau, are of special importance because of their unusually high timber values. These lands are in 18 counties in western Oregon in alternate sections, checker-boarded with national-forest and private tracts. Congress in 1937 established for the O&C lands a policy of sustained-yield timber management.[39] A substantial sale business with conservative cutting is being carried on. They are generally given good fire protection through cooperative associations or the Forest Service. Active effort is being made to organize cooperative sustained-yield units with owners of intermingled lands.

More than 16 million acres—about 40 percent commercial—is administered in trust for the Indians by the Office of Indian Affairs. Timber-sale policies aim at maximum financial returns consistent with good silviculture and watershed protection. Forest ranges are also under management. In general, protection and management are believed to approximate national-forest practices, especially in the West.

The national parks and monuments, administered by the National Park Service of the Department of the Interior, include about 7 million acres of forest land possessing outstanding scenic, historic, or scientific values. Commercial use of timber and most other products is excluded. The forests are kept in natural condition and hence afford good watershed protection and serve as important wildlife refuges.

Other Federal forest lands, totaling about 2 million acres, are administered by the Reclamation Service and the Fish and Wildlife Service of the Interior Department, the Soil Conservation Service of the Department of Agriculture, the military departments, and other agencies. Some, like the lands in military reservations and those acquired in farm resettlement purchases, are subject to transfer or other disposal. Others such as wildlife areas are under permanent management for purposes other than timber growing. Most, however, are in varying degree protected and under conservative management.

State and local governments own or manage under lease nearly 38 million acres of forest land, about two-thirds in the North and most of the remainder in the West:

[39] Act approved August 28, 1937 (50 Stat. 874).

	State and local government ownership of forest land, 1945 [1] (million acres)		
Section:	State	Local	Total
North	16.3	8.3	24.6
South	2.4	.2	2.6
West	8.7	1.9	10.6
United States	27.4	10.4	37.8

[1] Includes lands under long-term lease from the Federal Government.

They are increasing their holdings. Lands under State administration have grown from 19 million acres in 1938 to nearly 28 million in 1945 through purchase, lease, and taking over tax-reverted properties.

Some 38 States have a policy of establishing and managing State forests. A good proportion of the State lands has been blocked up as State forests, parks, or game refuges. Much, however, remains in scattered unorganized tracts, a great deal of it tax-reverted and in an uncertain ownership and management status. Lack of clear-cut policies handicaps a number of States in putting these lands in productive condition.

Administration and use both vary greatly. Nearly all State forest lands are protected against fire and trespass. Management, particularly of recreational resources, is in some cases good although many essential facilities are lacking. Timber management is excellent in some States, and on the average distinctly better than on private lands.

The expansion of State forests in recent years has found many State forestry agencies badly underequipped to do the work required of them. Some are hard-pressed to provide even the minimum of fire protection and to keep up roads, fire towers, and other facilities built and formerly maintained with the help of the Civilian Conservation Corps. To put State forest lands under satisfactory management, and particularly to get the 18 million acres of commercial forest into planned timber production, is difficult with present facilities. Fortunately forest administration is being strengthened in some States.

Local-government forest lands are a growing class and, in some respects, closest to the people. Despite the rather small acreage, they are contributing to the forestry movement, especially in New England and the Lake States. Of some 10 million acres, chiefly commercial, which is owned by counties, municipalities, schools, and other local public

· 4. Forest lands vital to control and use of water, where private ownership cannot assure good water-shed management.

5. Forests of high value for recreation, wildlife propagation, and other public services, where private ownership will not afford adequate development or access.·

6. Lands so intermingled with or integrally related to public forests that their separate ownership seriously hampers administration and management of the public lands.

Of high priority is the acquisition of a large acreage in the last category—the intermingled lands. In the West, much national-forest and other Federal land forms a checkered pattern of alternate mile-square sections, interspersed with private and other holdings that were alienated in this fashion from the public domain. Within the exterior boundaries of other national forests, the pattern of ownership is somewhat similarly patchy, though not in a regular checkerboard (fig. 29). In some units of the eastern national forests, Federal ownership constitutes less than half of the total. Within the boundaries of all national forests, there are nearly 50 million acres of alienated land of which, it is estimated, some 35 million should be acquired. Some State forests are similarly broken up, and many are in small, widely scattered units.

Patchwork ownership adds to the difficulties in protecting forests, in laying out satisfactory road systems, in managing timber and other resources; and, indeed, in exercising most management functions. Although cooperative management of public and private lands under sustained-yield agreements [41] will meet the needs in some localities, consolidation through purchase or exchange is the chief means of unscrambling the jigsaw pattern which so often impedes effective administration of public forests.·

Progress in acquisition has been much too slow. This reflects public apathy—mostly lack of understanding of forestry needs and of what public forests can contribute to local economic and industrial welfare. Then, too, there is opposition in some localities motivated by fear of government encroachment into private affairs. On the other hand, local interest and initiative are responsible for much public acquisition. As yet, the general public is not well informed of its large stake in stable, effective management of forest land on

[41] See p. 94.

91

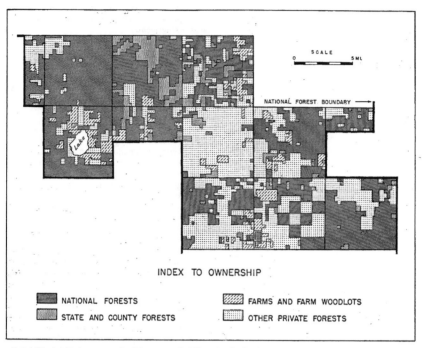

SCALE
0   5 ML

NATIONAL FOREST BOUNDARY ⟶

INDEX TO OWNERSHIP

| NATIONAL FORESTS | FARMS AND FARM WOODLOTS |
| STATE AND COUNTY FORESTS | OTHER PRIVATE FORESTS |

FIGURE 29.—*A typical eastern national-forest area, in Wisconsin, showing intermingled ownership. Such patchy holdings usually are difficult to administer.*

which public values are paramount or where private forestry is clearly a losing game.

Opposition to enlarging the national forests is often based on the effect of public ownership on local tax revenues. This usually overlooks the indirect benefits and pay rolls which national-forest protection and development bring to the local communities. It also overlooks the fact that to a large extent acquisition involves cut-over or low-value lands, much of which would yield little tax revenue had they remained in private ownership. Yet it is evident that Federal financial contributions to local governments on account of Federal ownership should be put on a more uniform and stable basis. At present there is no consistent contribution policy; in some instances no Federal payment at all is made.

The national forests pay 25 percent of gross receipts to the States for redistribution to the counties in which the forests are located.[42] In addition 10 percent of the receipts are appropriated for construction of roads and trails in these counties.[43] This generally affords adequate returns to local government, especially since there have been very substantial increases in national-forest receipts in recent years. However, there are local inequities, particularly where the tax base is limited and where forest land is so depleted that it will yield only nominal revenue for many years.

A main difficulty is that the present system of

[42] For the year ending June 30, 1947, the contribution to some 653 counties totaled more than 4.5 million dollars.

[43] For the year ending June 30, 1947, the road fund amounted to 1.8 million dollars.

ingly small part of the private commercial forest. Lumber manufacturers own some 37 million acres or 11 percent, about three-fourths in medium and large holdings. Nearly 45 percent of lumber-company lands are in the South, about 40 percent in the West.

Pulp manufacturers own about 14.5 million acres or 4 percent, nearly all in medium and large holdings. More than 95 percent is in the East.

Some 43 million acres—about half of all medium and large holdings—are owned by a great variety of individuals and companies other than lumber and pulp manufacturers.

	Private commercial forest land	
	Million acres	Percent
Ownership class:		
Small holdings (5,000 acres or less):		
Farm	[1]136	40
Other	[2]125	35
Total	261	76
Medium and large holdings (more than 5,000 acres):		
Lumber company	27	8
Pulp company	14	4
Other	43	12
Total	84	24
All private	345	100

[1] Total acreage on farms is 139 million acres, 3 million in holdings larger than 5,000 acres.

[2] Includes 10 million acres of lumber-company holdings; about 0.5 million of pulp-company lands.

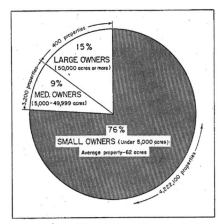

FIGURE 30.—*Ownership of the 345 million acres of private commercial forest land, by size of holding.*

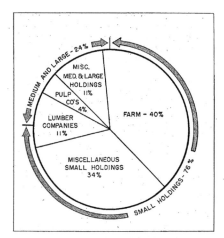

FIGURE 31.—*Distribution of private commercial forest land by class of ownership.*

Whatever the class of ownership, there is ample evidence that private forestry pays and is good business. The more profitable opportunities occur where timber grows fast and markets are favorable, and particularly where there is enough accessible growing stock to operate with continuous revenue. The South, with its rapid timber growth, now offers the best example. In the North, good markets are a special advantage. Throughout the country, a growing number of owners have started the practice of forestry. Today this movement is favored by high prices. Although no cause for jubilation from the public point of view because they are a symptom of timber scarcity, high prices should be helpful in powering the take-off of a larger forestry movement.

Private forestry, however, has many obstacles, some of which are implicit in the small size of holdings. Furthermore, the means and ability of owners to practice good forestry vary widely.

Larger Owners Have Some Advantages

Of the 84 million acres in 3,600 medium and large properties, the 41 million of pulp- and lumber-company lands especially lend themselves to good forestry. Their owners usually have the facilities including the financial strength needed to undertake sustained-yield forestry, granted the in-

tent to practice it and the aim to keep mills and plants operating on a permanent basis. Much progress is being made. Yet even here, the fact that four-tenths of the cutting is poor or destructive (see p. 49) shows that many of these lands still lack stable, proposeful management.

Lumber-company ownership of forests is still exploitive in many instances. Generally, however, it has in recent years been becoming more stable. Today the objective of many owners is to integrate woods and mill for permanent operation. The number of operators who have achieved this seems to be increasing. Balance is being gained through measures to increase the allowable cut of timber—rehabilitating cut-over lands, managing and protecting merchantable areas, and acquiring more lands. In some cases balance is being sought also through scaling down and modernizing plant facilities.

Cooperation between public and private owners to pool holdings into sustained-yield units will help stabilize lumber enterprises and the communities dependent on them. The sustained-yield unit act of 1944,[44] authorizes agreements between the Secretary of Agriculture and willing private or public forest owners for sustained-yield management of interrelated national-forest and other lands. In return for committing his lands to a coordinated management plan, the operator can purchase national-forest timber without competition at the appraised value. The Act gives similar authority to the Secretary of the Interior with respect to lands under his jurisdiction.

One unit has been set up by the Secretary of Agriculture, and negotiations are under way for several others. It is tentatively estimated that from 20 to 25 percent of the commercial area of the national forests eventually might be included in such units.

The pulp industry—with heavy long-term investment in plant and equipment, dependence upon a steady flow of pulpwood, and ability to use small trees—is making the best showing in private forestry. The pulp industry's southward movement has been attended by acquisition of much southern pine forest. About two-thirds of pulp-company lands are under at least extensive management (see pp. 50–51), but there is still a big forestry job to be done in building up their productivity.

The 43 million acres of large and medium properties not in lumber- or pulp-company ownership

---

[44] Act approved March 29, 1944 (58 Stat. 132).

Miscellaneous Publication 668, U. S. Department of Agriculture

are held by a variety of individuals and companies: Railroads, mining and land concerns, large estates, institutional and private investors, speculators, and even a few farmers. Policies are diverse and usually not conducive to good forestry. In the case of railroad, mining-company, and some institutional or estate forests, ownership—though incidental to other aims—is reasonably stable. Here there is usually a sound basis for good forestry though the opportunities for the most part are going begging. In many other instances ownership—by banks, mortgagors, private investors, and the like—is temporary and affords poor prospect for private forestry. Yet even temporary owners have a stake in protection and other measures that would safeguard their investment.

In assessing the progress by larger owners one question naturally arises: Whence has come the upturn in forestry practice and is it permanent? The declining supply of timber, growing public awareness of the seriousness of the forest situation, and a tendency to associate destructive practices with large-scale private ownership doubtless have been important factors. Spurred on by such considerations, the timber-trade and other industrial associations have publicized forest conservation and have encouraged members to put it into practice.

But the present movement has gained momentum largely because of the favorable economic climate in which these forces have operated. Demand and prices for forest products have been high. Forest-land prices in many cases have until recently been low. High income-tax rates have, in effect, reduced the net cost of expenditures for forestry. The whole movement may mark the beginning of a long upward trend. Or it may level off if economic conditions become less favorable.

Despite these encouraging advances, the fact remains that more than half the land in medium and large holdings is without purposeful forestry management.[45] There are as yet few examples of private timber growing where long waiting is involved. A waxing private interest in forest conservation where market and growth conditions are favorable should not obscure the unmet challenge of many millions of other acres whose output is needed to help fill the Nation's wood box but whose depleted condition or small return is unattractive to private enterprise unless heavy public support is forthcoming.

[45] See section How Timberlands Are Being Managed, pp. 46–51.

Small Forest Owners: The Heart of the Problem

The more formidable obstacles in private forestry center, however, on the more than 4 million small properties which total about three-fourths of the private land. Their large number and small size, the variable aims and skill with which they are handled, and the unstable ownership and management of many—these are knotty factors which long have blocked efforts to get forest conservation into more general practice.

The 139 million acres of farm woods are held largely in conjunction with property managed for other purposes. To the individual farmer, his woodland is usually a minor resource. Yet farm woodland is the largest category of forest land, and hence is of great national importance.

Farm ownership generally affords a favorable setting for forestry. It is comparatively stable and enables a maximum of on-the-ground managerial attention. Farm forestry requires little cash outlay. Mostly it utilizes time not fully employed on other farm jobs.

Public policy has long sought to make woodland management an integral part of the farm business. However, such management is not yet extensively practiced. With the greatest opportunities for intensive forestry, farmers still lack, as a class, the knowledge and incentives to practice it. Even with the advances that have been made in aiding farm forestry—in education, technical assistance, and incentive payments—most farm woodlands are still the back yard of the farm, subjected to thoughtless cutting, pasturing, and burning.

The 125 million acres of other small holdings are in many respects a more difficult problem. They have received little if any attention in aid programs, yet are an inseparable part of the agricultural problem of rural people and of rural land. Furthermore, forestry on both nonfarm and farm properties is beset by similar handicaps which call for much the same remedial program.

The small nonfarm woodlands, like the larger properties, are held by people and companies of the widest diversity of purposes as owners. Many become owners by default, by inheritance, or in some other fortuitous manner. Some have put money into timber. Some are sawmill operators. Many are investors in minerals or in potential farming sites, and the forest to them is secondary. Still others hold the land for a variety of purposes, some for reasons of sentiment. The great majority are absentee owners.

A major handicap, as with the farmer owner, is lack of forestry know-how—of how to grow, harvest, and market timber to best advantage. Most small owners and operators lack the experience to perform or supervise these tasks expertly. They need much technical information and on-the-ground assistance in forest management. Here there is constructive opportunity for public aid on a greatly enlarged scale.

Small size, of itself, also entails handicaps. Small holdings, particularly if badly depleted, may be commensurate neither with the income needs of the owner nor with the labor and other investments he might put into them. Small size usually means that the operator grows, harvests, and markets timber as a side line. As a seller, he often is unable to reach good markets. With small output and returns, there is little incentive to practice good timber management.

The cooperative association long used by farmers in overcoming the handicaps of smallness has application to forestry. Since the first "forest cooperative" was organized in this country, more than 40 years ago, the movement has shown sporadic growth. Many associations have failed. A few have had long and successful histories. During the past 10 years or so there appear to have been some 57 forest-cooperative associations of different types, but engaged chiefly in marketing farm timber. Most are in the Lake and other northern States where farm cooperatives have prospered. Some handle timber only; some, as a side line to farm commodities. At least one processes the timber of members before selling the products. Some also provide timber-management service and require adherence to good cutting practices.[46]

Forest cooperatives, given needed encouragement by public agencies, should help to meet the problems of the small forest owner.

Closely associated with small size is low income. There is many a small property, farm and nonfarm, whose owner or operator is hard-pressed financially and which has been picked over for every bit of income it will yield. In most of these cases the forest is shorn of merchantable timber and will not produce much for many years. Meanwhile the poverty of the owner perpetuates the poverty of

his forest; he cannot afford to postpone what little income there is while growing stock is being built up.

Such very low-income forest properties, it is roughly estimated, total about 65 million acres or one-fourth of the commercial land in small holdings. These are concentrated in the more depressed rural areas, where natural and industrial resources are limited: the Piedmont and Coastal Plain of the South, the southern and central highlands from the Appalachians to the Ozarks, and the northern Lake States.

There are no simple solutions to the tough problem of rehabilitating these small, low-income properties in the face of the economic pressures which keep them depleted. Rehabilitation in any event will be slow and will involve recreating the people's whole resource base so as to raise their total income. In the more depressed areas, it is improbable that growing stock can be restored while there is still a heavy population on the land and the forests remain in private ownership.

Absentee ownership is another serious obstacle.[47] When an owner leaves his property unoccupied or turns it over to a tenant, good forest management is doubly difficult to attain.

Despite the poor showing by small holdings as a class, there is opportunity for forestry on a large proportion of them. But the present picture is largely one of mismanagement, of exploitation on millions of small properties adding up to exploitation on a grand scale. The picture reveals serious handicaps, economic and physical, to satisfactory forestry. It reveals the heavy handicap of sheer lack of knowledge of forestry and its possibilities. Yet if private forestry is to do the job it needs to do, it must prove itself on these small holdings as well as on the larger ones—for in these is three-fourths of the private commercial forest. The small property is indeed the crux of our forest problem.

Some Economic Factors Affecting Private Forestry

The job in private forestry is one of getting permanent sustained-yield management that will not only profit the owner but also serve the public interest. The public's part of the job is largely a

<hr />

46 Fuller discussion is given in Reappraisal Report 6, Forest Cooperatives in the United States. U. S. Dept. Agr., Forest Service. 1947.

47 In the 26 States east of the Mississippi River, where nearly three-fourths of all farm woodland is concentrated, 36 percent of the farms are operated by tenants.

matter of minimizing the handicaps—of making private forestry more attractive, and helping private owners see and make the most of their opportunities. It also involves protecting the heavy investments which the public should shoulder in helping to spread good private forestry.

Some of the more obvious needs such as better forest protection, more technical assistance in forestry, and the like, are implicit in the difficulties confronting private owners—especially those relating to small properties. But there are several other things that affect ownership and management of private forests:

First, there is need for adequate financing. Forestry is a long-time enterprise. It involves long-term investments—not merely the capital for year-to-year operation but that required to build up a satisfactory growing stock.

The problem of waiting—of financial forbearance —is no small one. For example, the lumber company with high-interest-rate loans on mature forest may have to choose between liquidation or default. The timber operator who gets capital at high cost from the buyers of his product may find himself forced into exploitive practices. The private timber owner, especially the small one, usually must put his need for current income ahead of long-run considerations. To all these, waiting is expensive —often too expensive to afford.

The problem of financing private forests also includes making needed adjustments—enlarging timber holdings to economical operating size; planting, stand improvement, and other measures; revamping of road or mill layout; and the like. All this calls for financing at reasonable cost. The chief need is low-interest-rate credit for periods ranging up to 40 or even 60 years while growing stock is being built up. Some loans are needed to finance operations or improvements that will pay off more quickly.

Forest owners and operators generally lack sources of satisfactory credit—long-term or intermediate-adapted to their special needs. Today, when specialized credit facilities for farming and for industry have been developed to a high state of efficiency by both public and private agencies, forestry is the outstanding category where credit needs remain neglected.

Second, there is need for forest insurance. Risks from fire, insects, disease, and other destructive agents are not only reducible but also insurable. Forest insurance is well established in several European countries. But in this country, although commercial companies have given considerable attention to the possibilities and have written some policies at high rates, forest insurance has been slow to catch on. Studies in the Pacific Northwest and the Northeast [48] indicate that commercial insurance is practicable at reasonable rates if it avoids poor risks and is based on good protection, reasonably good forest practices, and broad coverage.

Third, property taxes have long been regarded as a major obstacle to private forestry. Annual taxes, to be sure, may encourage premature cutting or abandonment of young or cut-over forests. Furthermore, the fact that taxes are considered an obstacle tends to make them so.

However, the effect of property taxes as a deterrent to forestry has generally been exaggerated. Management of farm woods, for example, is little affected because they are seldom taxed separately from the rest of the farm and the costs chargeable to them are rarely segregated. Less than half the private land is likely to be influenced in its management by property taxes, and only a fraction of this probably is appreciably affected.

An important factor in the tax burden is poor administration. Inequities in assessment as between forest and other land, as well as unpredictable fluctuations in the tax, create special burdens on forest owners. High costs of local government complicate the problem, especially where forests are the main tax base and depletion is widespread. Some of these burdens are being lightened. Many States are giving increasing help to local governments in making more uniform and equitable assessments. Some States are assuming the support of roads, schools, and other services formerly borne by counties and districts, and some have limited the local tax rates by statute. Between 1932 and 1941, costs of State and local government rose from 8.5 to 12.8 billion dollars, but property taxes remained at about 4.5 billion dollars. Meanwhile tax delinquency, a sensitive barometer, has fallen to a long-time low.

Even so, forest taxation remains much in the public eye as indicated by the continuing stream of legislation. As of 1946 twenty-six States had special forest-tax laws on the books. Mostly this is ex-

[48] SHEPARD, H. B. FOREST FIRE INSURANCE IN THE PACIFIC COAST STATES. U. S. Dept. Agri. Tech. Bul. 551, 168 pp., illus. 1937.
———. FOREST FIRE INSURANCE IN THE NORTHEASTERN STATES. U. S. Dept. Agr. Tech. Bul. 651, 46 pp., illus. 1939.

emption and yield-tax legislation of the optional variety.[49] which has proved largely ineffective. In no State is more than 8 percent of the private commercial forest land classified under such laws, and in more than half less than 1 percent. Only two States, Ohio and Washington, have differential or deferred forest taxation [50] of the type recommended by the Forest Service more than 10 years ago.[51]

That Federal and State income taxes seriously hamper good forest practice is doubtful because they do not reach the great mass of owners, nor those who are making no net income. Indeed, the high tax rates of recent years may have encouraged concerns with high income to spend more for forestry. State and Federal estate taxes occasionally have some adverse influence, but most forest properties, including those of corporations, are not subject to them and few are subject to upper-bracket rates.

Public Interest in Private Forests Should Be Safeguarded

To keep all forest land reasonably productive, there is need for some public restraints upon cutting and other practices on lands in private ownership. The public should set up common-sense rules that will prevent clear-cutting without provision for restocking, stop unnecessary destruction of young growth, and require reasonable safeguards with respect to fire, grazing, and logging.

This is an essential step to assure sound private forestry. Owners, large and small, have a vital stake in the kind of forestry practiced on each other's land since "cut-out-and-get-out" practices have a direct bearing on the stability and strength of local markets which are so advantageous to profitable private forestry. Indeed, good cutting practices, such as are already being attained on many private holdings, are in the long run one of the best guarantees of vigor and permanence of

[49] Provides for exclusion of immature timber from the property-tax base or for substitution of a severance tax; optional in the sense that the taxpayer takes the initiative in enrolling his timber under provisions of the law, but is not required to do so.

[50] In differential taxation, a flat percentage reduction is applied to the assessed value or tax rate of forest lands. In deferred taxation, the tax bill is postponed (and usually accumulates at interest).

[51] HALL, R. C. THE FOREST-TAX PROBLEM AND ITS SOLUTION SUMMARIZED. U. S. Dept. Agr. Cir. 358, 17 pp. 1935. Pp. 14–17.

industries and communities, as well as of the forestry enterprises that sustain them.

Basically, the need for regulation stems from the large responsibility to safeguard forest values in the interests of society as a whole. The authority of government to impose reasonable restrictions on personal and property rights of individuals to prevent injury to the public welfare is a widely accepted principle of law. This is reflected by a large and growing body of regulatory laws—Federal, State, and local—of which there are many commonplace examples: Speed laws, zoning ordinances, sanitation and building codes; and regulations affecting such broad fields as commerce, transportation, public health, and conservation and use of national resources. The public, to whom private forestry looks increasingly for financial aid and other services, needs some minimum guarantee, such as regulation affords, that forest lands will be kept productive and that its large investment will be protected.

Regulation of private forest practices has in recent years won considerable acceptance in principle, although there is also much opposition to it and much controversy about whether it should be State or Federal. Nowhere as yet, in this country, is it on a satisfactory basis. Some 14 States now have regulatory laws on their books, 3 of them enacted prior to 1925 and 10 in or since 1940. Since 1940, unsuccessful efforts have been made in 10 other States to pass regulatory laws.

Some of the laws specify definite rules of practice: usually that seed trees be kept or that the cutting be limited by diameter. A majority place responsibility on a single State agency, which is a requisite of good administration. Less than half, however, provide for the needed advice and assistance to forest owners and operators. Only a few are believed to provide adequately for enforcement. In most, the silvicultural standards require little or no improvement in the prevalent cutting practices. In some States the law is to all intents and purposes a dead letter.

There are many obstacles to getting effective regulation, Nation-wide, based solely on State-by-State action. Progress would be exceedingly slow. Some States might not act at all. And results doubtless would be spotty. They would probably vary from very little in some States to a good job in some financially strong States with good laws and effective enforcement. Regulation probably would be poorest in extensively forested States where it ought

3. How to equip public forests so that they may contribute more, as they must, to our national supply of timber and other forest products and to other services.

Clearly, much remains to be done in formulating and implementing national policies with respect to the public's stake and responsibilities in private forestry; in providing effective protection against fire and other hazards; in making readily available the technical know-how and essential on-the-ground management services; in helping private owners to overcome the handicaps of small-scale operation, unfamiliarity with technical forestry methods, and difficulty in financing forest enterprises; and in strengthening and enlarging public forests.

These are the issues to be met. For the Nation needs productive forests. Timber is a basic and indispensable natural resource—an important part of America's great industrial strength. But our timber supply is running dangerously low. We are overdrawing our forest bank account and new growth is falling far short of prospective requirements. A much stronger program of forestry is needed to assure timber for the future and to care for the expanding needs of watershed protection, forest recreation, and other forest uses. If the United States is to maintain a place of economic leadership in the world of tomorrow, it can ill afford to temporize with its forests.

☆U. S. GOVERNMENT PRINTING OFFICE: 1948— 806034

CPSIA information can be obtained
at www.ICGtesting.com
Printed in the USA
BVHW041123261118
534012BV00020B/886/P

9 780364 675762